Letters To A Brot[illegible] [illegible]riest

co-authored by Rev. [illegible] [illegible]cia

and Rev. Msgr. [illegible]

Letters for everyone on the love of Jesus in the Blessed Sacrament.

A truly inspirational bestseller!

Nihil Obstat: **Msgr. J.C. Abriol**

MISSIONARIES OF CHARITY

"As long as you did it to one of these My least brethren. You did it to Me"

Calcutta, 15th Aug. 1993

Dear Father

Perpetual Adoration with exposition needs a great push. People ask me: "What will convert America and save the world? My answer is prayer. What we need is for every Parish to come before Jesus in the Blessed Sacrament in holy hours of Prayer.

I pray that the Community Missionaries of the Blessed Sacrament dedicated to this purpose of spreading perpetual adoration will flourish

I want every member to know that this Community has my whole hearted support and encouragement.

Let us do all things all for Jesus through Mary

God bless you

M Teresa MC

MOTHER TERESA, MC

"I hope that this form of Perpetual Adoration, with permanent exposition of the Blessed Sacrament will continue into the future. Specifically, I hope that the fruit of this Congress results in the establishment of Perpetual Eucharistic Adoration in all parishes and Christian communities throughout the world," from Pope John Paul II's June 1993 homily at the 45th International Eucharistic Congress in Seville, Spain.

Pope John II being presented with a photo album of over one hundred chapels of Perpetual Adoration in Korea after the International Congress at which the Pope visited one of the chapels and stated that it was most fitting "that his first stop at the Congress be a chapel of Perpetual Adoration at the parish of the Good Shepherd."

"The best the surest and the most effective way of establishing everlasting peace on the face of the earth is through the great power of Perpetual Adoration of the Blessed Sacrament,"

words of Pope John Paul II in establishing Perpetual Eucharistic Adoration with Exposition on December 2, 1981 at St. Peter's in Rome.

Spiritual leaders praise Letters To A Brother Priest:

"The Meditations are valuable, because they broaden the horizons of our thinking about the Holy Eucharist. We need to awaken to the beauty and the depth of this great Mystery of our Faith. For those who want to increase their faith and love for Jesus in this Sacrament, this book will be a real blessing," *Most Reverend Donald W. Montrose, Bishop of Stockton, CA.*

"Letters To A Brother Priest helps us to better understand the beauty and power of the Blessed Sacrament in the culmination of God's plan in Salvation History," *Ricardo J. Cardinal Vidal, Archbishop of Cebu.*

"The value of a single holy hour of prayer, the worth of one chapel of Perpetual Adoration is beyond our capability to think, imagine, or even desire," *Jaime L. Cardinal Sin, Archbishop of Manila.*

"These letters are a message of hope," *Msgr. Moises Andrade, Professor of Liturgy, Quezon City, Manila.*

"I think that if enough young priests like myself would stand up, speak out and be heard, there would be a more zealous Church for the cause of Christ in the Blessed Sacrament," *Fr. Thomas Naval.*

"It is with this profound faith that I fervently pray that from the Philippines, Perpetual Adoration will spread throughout the world through the Missionaries of the Blessed Sacrament," *President of the Philippines, Corazon Aquino.*

"What the world needs now is another revolution or a second Pentecost, one leading all humanity to the Heart of Jesus in the Blessed Sacrament," *Vice President of the Philippines, Salvador Laurel.*

"Perpetual Adoration with exposition needs a great push. People ask me: 'What will convert America and save the world?' My answer is prayer. What we need is for every Parish to come before Jesus in the Blessed Sacrament in holy hours of prayer," *Mother Teresa.*

Cardinal's Residence
P. O. Box 52
Cebu City 6000
Philippines

MESSAGE

When I see the poverty, the disease, and the pain in the world today, my heart aches for suffering humanity. If I can feel this way, how much more so is the Heart of God moved by the cry of His children? I am sure that God wants to put an end to this period of trial and tribulation. He wants to establish his Kingdom of peace and justice, but He is waiting for us to do our part. If we are willing only to do what is ordinary,then we can only expect God's ordinary blessings. Only when we are willing to do the extraordinary are we guaranteed of obtaining God's extraordinary blessings.

Perpetual adoration of the Blessed Sacrament is absolutely the extraordinary effort that God is asking for today in order that He may bestow upon mankind His extraordinary blessings. When we are willing to do on earth what is done in heaven, ie., adore God perpetually, then God will create a "new heaven" and a "new earth".

This is the message of the Blessed Mother: The triumph of the Immaculate Heart of Mary will be the Eucharistic Reign of Her Son. And the Eucharistic reign of Jesus through perpetual adoration in every parish will bring about the New Era.

Jesus will claim His Kingdom only when we proclaim Him King by giving Him the love and honor He truly deserves and desires through perpetual adoration.

I admire the many priests throughout the world who have perpetual adoration in their parishes and the many bishops who encourage it in their dioceses. I cannot understand why anyone should question it. The only one who would not want Jesus to be adored day and night, and the only one who would do anything to prevent it, is Satan himself.

Perpetual adoration of the Blessed Sacrament is the solution to our problems of declining vocations, disintegrating families, and the defection of many of our brethren to fundamentalist sects.

Perpetual adoration is a clarion call to our people to develop a personal relationship with Jesus, our Savior, who is present in Person in the most Blessed Sacrament.

We should be the one to challenge our people to come to where Jesus is, truly present in the Blessed Sacrament. Anyone who truly appreciates the gift of the Holy Eucharist would never think of leaving the Catholic Church.

Unfortunately, the scene today is right out of Scripture: "The priests asked not, 'Where is the Lord? . . . Be amazed at this, O heavens, and shudder with sheer horror,' says the Lord. 'Two evils have my people done. They have forsaken me, the source of living waters. They have dug themselves cisterns, broken cisterns that hold no water.'" (Jer. 2:8a,12 and 13)

Through perpetual adoration Jesus wants to make an orchard out of a desert. This is why Msgr. Ramirez's book is so important and why I want each of my priests to have a copy. Letters To A Brother Priest helps us to better understand the beauty and the power of the Blessed Sacrament in the culmination of God's plan in salvation history.

The book mentions the work of Bishop Felix Zafra and Fr. Martin Lucia, who together founded a community of priests called Missionaries of the Blessed Sacrament. This commendable work marks an initial step towards the establishment of Christ's Eucharistic reign. But much more needs to be done.

I fervently pray that this book will inspire every priest to have perpetual adoration of the Blessed Sacrament in their parish. Then will Christ be truly worshipped in every corner of the earth.

+RICARDO J. CARDINAL VIDAL
Archbishop of Cebu

RICARDO J. CARDINAL VIDAL
Archbishop of Cebu

The Roman Catholic Archbishop of Manila
121 Arzobispo Street, Intramuros
P. O. Box 132
Manila, Philippines

Message from Cardinal Sin

On more than one occasion I have said it, and I want to say it again. Perpetual adoration is the pastoral consolation and joy of my apostolic efforts in the Archdiocese.

For this reason, I am happy that these letters from Msgr. Josefino S. Ramirez to Fr. Thomas Naval are being published. His soul is printed on each page. That we have a Eucharistic diocese with over one hundred chapels of perpetual adoration is a great credit to the time, the planning, and the zeal Msgr. Ramirez has demonstrated since the very beginning when I first invited Fr. Martin Lucia to the Philippines to promote perpetual adoration.

The great importance of devotion to the Blessed Sacrament was emphatically stated by Pope John Paul II at the International Eucharistic Congress in Seville, Spain last June 1993. The Pope prayed that "the fruit of the congress be the establishment of perpetual adoration in every parish and Christian community throughout the world." On Holy Thursday of 1994, the Congregation for the Clergy published the Directory on the Ministry and Life of Priests. This document gives new impetus to perpetual adoration when it proclaims "faith and love for the Eucharist will not allow Christ to remain alone in His Presence" and challenges each priest to be a model for the faithful in Eucharistic adoration.

I want to take this opportunity to thank the pastors and priests of the Archdiocese for the great love they have expressed for Our Eucharistic Lord by providing chapels of perpetual adoration for the laity.

May the faithful also be inspired by these letters. May their commitment to their holy hour be deepened and their joy in being with the Blessed Sacrament be enhanced.

The value of a single holy hour of prayer, the worth of one chapel of perpetual adoration is beyond our capability to think, imagine, or even desire. It reminds me of a story I read in the newspaper about a married couple in Europe who inherited a house from a deceased relative. In the house was an old painting of a flower pot. They were going to throw it out in the process of cleaning the house for a dinner party they were having for a few friends.

One of the friends worked at a museum and became curious about the old painting on the wall, as the couple forgot to throw it out. He took the painting back to the museum to have it examined. There it was discovered it was not a copy but an original Vincent Van Gogh. Thus worth many millions of dollars, making them one of the wealthiest couples in all of Europe.

Your daily holy hour and chapel of perpetual adoration is worth far more than you think it is. Like the young couple, you will be astounded, eternally astounded, when you discover in heaven exactly how much more.

Devoutly Yours in Christ,

+ Jaime Card. Sin

+ JAIME L. CARDINAL SIN
Archbishop of Manila

SALVADOR H. LAUREL
Vice-President of the Philippines

Fr. Thomas with Msgr. Pepe

ALAGAD NI MARIA

PRELATURE OF INFANTA

Infanta, Quezon, Philippines

Introduction from Fr. Thomas

To My Brother Priests,

I have known Msgr. Ramirez since I was eleven years old. He was very instrumental in my vocation to the priesthood.

I have always appreciated his efforts to help me to be a happy and holy priest. For this reason I saved the letters he wrote me, letters like an elder brother to a younger brother. If any one of these thirty letters of inspiration helps a single priest come to know Jesus better in the Blessed Sacrament, then the effort to have them published would be most worthwhile. It may be best to read just one a day, like a mini-thirty day retreat, rather than read them all at once like a book.

One day I was thinking that these letters may help others as they have helped me. I was too shy and embarrassed to give serious consideration to having them published. Then I thought that today is not the time to consider oneself.

There is too much silence already. I would love to do my part in beginning a new trend. Maybe I am just too young to know better. I think that if enough young priests like myself would stand up, speak out and be heard, there would be a more zealous Church for the cause of Christ in the Blessed Sacrament.

What is presently a negative attitude toward the Blessed Sacrament could become a positive attitude if only we would be willing to be more courageous, going from whispering to witnessing.

I would love to do my part in starting a world-wide movement, a movement without any name or dues, a movement of priests, not tentative but manly, for the cause of Christ in the Blessed Sacrament.

At the first Eucharist, Christ was betrayed for thirty pieces of silver. All of the apostles scattered, even Peter did not know Him.

Now is the time for all of us to return and say we know Him. We know Jesus in the Blessed Sacrament. We love Jesus in the Blessed Sacrament. Our life is dedicated to His Eucharistic Reign.

May His Kingdom Come,

Fr. Thomas K. Naval

Fr. Thomas Naval

MAILING ADDRESS: QCC P.O. BOX 1539 ZIP CODE 1155 QUEZON CITY, PHILIPPINES

FOREWORD

> "In the Most Blessed Eucharist is contained the whole spiritual good of the Church, namely Christ Himself our Pasch. For this reason, the Eucharist appears as the source and summit of all preaching of the Gospel." (Vatican Council II)

The focus of the post-conciliar Church is on the centrality of the Holy Eucharist with an emphasis on evangelization. Thus, eucharistic evangelization is at the forefront of the Church's mission and the main thrust of authentic apostolic activity.

These letters written by Msgr. Josefino Ramirez are in keeping with the focus of the Church and should inspire us all to the greater appreciation of the power and love of the Blessed Sacrament. The second Vatican Council encouraged daily visits to the Blessed Sacrament. "As a help towards faithful fulfillment of their ministry, priests should love to talk daily with Christ the Lord in their visit to the Blessed Sacrament and in their personal devotion to it." (Life of Priests)

As recent as Holy Thursday 1994, the Congregation for the Clergy reexpressed the centrality of the Holy Eucharist in a document entitled Directory on the Ministry and Life of Priests in which each priest is called upon to be a MODEL FOR THE FAITHFUL in Eucharistic Adoration: "The centrality of the Eucharist should be apparent not only in the worthy celebration of the sacrifice, but also in the proper adoration of the sacrament so that the priest might be the model for the faithful."

For this reason, I pray that every priest will read this book as it helps us understand even better, the purpose, the value and the importance of the daily holy hour.

The best theology is not always the most complicated, difficult, or hardest to understand. The best theology is usually the most simple and easiest to understand since God is simplicity personified and theology is, after all, the study of God Himself.

Simplicity characterizes "Letters to a Brother Priest." Written by Msgr. Josefino Ramirez in a simple, down to earth style, these letters reflect the cheerful, warm and generous personality of the Vicar General of Manila.

Since the Eucharist is the sign and cause of unity, I am especially pleased to see the Providential hand of God in the implementation and cooperation of the spreading of Perpetual Adoration to all nations. That the history of the Missionaries of the Blessed Sacrament involves the harmonious working together of priests from the Philippines, United States and Australia and other nations, is a reflection on the Eucharist as the Sacrament of Unity. Through the grace of God and with the enthusiastic cooperation of many bishops and priests around the world, this new community has been able to establish over one thousand chapels of perpetual adoration in Catholic parishes located throughout five continents of the world. This effort has resulted in a Papal Decree which makes it emphatically clear that the church not only permits, but wholeheartedly encourages, perpetual adoration of the Blessed Sacrament exposed for the faithful in parishes. This Papal Decree came "after receiving the testimony of bishops of various countries who know, appreciate and encourage" devotion to Jesus in the Blessed Sacrament. (Papal Decree on Perpetual Adoration, June 2nd, 1991)

Without fear or intimidation, any parish priest has the pastoral right and joyful privilege to do all he can to bring all of those entrusted to his care to the Heart of Jesus through perpetual adoration: "Priests are to seek and perseveringly ask of God for the true spirit of adoration. By this spirit they themselves and with them the people entrusted to their care, will unite themselves with Christ the Mediator of the New Testament, and will be able as adopted sons to cry, "ABBA! FATHER!" (Rom. 8:15) (Vatican Council II)

These letters are a message of hope. Jesus is here now in the Blessed Sacrament waiting for us with open arms and will stay with us until the very end of time. Through the Blessed Sacrament Jesus will come again in glory and transform this world into a paradise. "Jesus will have a great surprise. He is living with His Mother among us. We will see Him in glory with rays of light. He will brighten the whole world with His rays. The last messages are beautiful - it's incredible the way He will come in glory." (Betania)

Originally, these letters were written to a young priest friend of the Monsignor. I personally want to thank the Monsignor for being willing to share them with all of us.

This book is a clarion call to all of us devoted to the Blessed Sacrament. We should all work together for Eucharistic Evangelization, that there may be a Eucharistic Renewal in the Church through Perpetual Adoration which will bring about the Eucharistic Reign of Christ and the New Era. "In the tender compassion of our God, the dawn from on High will break upon us, to shine on those living in darkness and in the shadow of death, and to guide our feet into the way of Peace." (Lk 1:78, 79)

MSGR. MOISES ANDRADE
Professor of Theology
Saint Vincent's Seminary

TABLE OF CONTENTS

BLESSED ARE THOSE WHO HAVE NOT SEEN AND HAVE BELIEVED

Feast Day of St. Thomas the Apostle
July 3, 1993

J.M.J.

Dear Fr. Thomas,

Happy feast day! Something very funny happened to me a couple of years ago. I was thinking about this when I decided to write to you. What happened was that Fr. Martin Lucia and I went on a retreat together. Since I had a bad cold and was coughing, Fr. Martin suggested that I take a drink of Cognac to help me sleep. I did not bring an alarm clock and I was concerned that if I took the drink, I would not be able to get up for my 3 a.m. holy hour with Our Lord in the Blessed Sacrament.

Fr. Martin assured me that God would find a way to get me up, so I took the drink. Bang! At 3 a.m., I heard this loud knocking and pounding on the door. Expecting Fr. Martin when I opened the door, I was most surprised when I looked down and saw a dog, instead. The dog had come into the house, went up the stairs, turned itself around, and slammed its tail against the door until I got up to open it. The next morning, I found out that the dog never goes inside the house.

So, I was just sitting here thinking to myself. If God can use a dog to bring me to my holy hour, can He not use me, dear Thomas, to bring you closer to the Blessed Sacrament? I want to keep writing you, pounding on my typewriter like that dog kept pounding on my door, until through the grace of God you start making a daily holy hour and have perpetual adoration in your parish.

It is a simple matter of faith; faith that the Blessed Sacrament is really Jesus in Person right here with us now! Your namesake did not believe that Jesus had risen, "unless I see the mark of the nails in His hands and put my finger into the nail marks and put my hand into His side, I will not believe." (Jn 20:25)

This is why he is called the "Doubting Thomas". Who is the "Doubting Thomas" today? People believe in the Resurrection, but do they know where Our Risen Savior dwells? The "Doubting Thomas" today is the one who does not believe that the Blessed Sacrament is Jesus, Our Risen Savior, with all of the power of His Resurrection flowing out to those who come into His Divine Presence!

Many would say "yes" they believe in the real presence. But faith is more than an intellectual assent. Belief is inseparable from behavior. If we believe that Jesus is present in the Blessed Sacrament, then we behave according to our belief. We go to Him, we come to Him, we run to Him. St. Paul says that: "Faith is confident assurance of what we hope for and conviction about those things we do not see." (HEB 11: 1)

Thomas, if you could see Jesus in the Blessed Sacrament, would you not set aside an hour each day to be with Him? If you could see Him as He really is, would you not have perpetual adoration in your parish? It would be impossible to stop it because the whole world would be coming day and night to see and be with Him.

Imagine what would happen if Jesus became visible in the Blessed Sacrament. Everyone in the world would want to catch the next flight to the Philippines and come to your parish. And would not Jesus say to each one what He said to Thomas the Apostle: "Have you come to believe because you have seen Me? Blessed are those who have not seen and have believed." (JN 20:28)

In today's gospel, Jesus appears to Thomas that he may believe that Christ has risen. A far greater wonder of His love is that He does not appear to you, my dear friend. Instead, Jesus waits for you in the Blessed Sacrament. He wants you to come to Him in faith that for all eternity He may call you "BLESSED".

He loves you too much to say: "Put your finger here and see my hands and bring your hand and put it into my side and do not be unbelieving, but believe." (JN 20:27)

Believe that the Blessed Sacrament is the same One who spoke these words to Thomas, the same Jesus who came through the locked doors and stood in the midst of the apostles and said: "PEACE BE WITH YOU."

This is the peace that Jesus wants you to experience in your holy hours of prayer. The experience of this peace is far better than Jesus showing you His wounds. His wounds in the Blessed Sacrament are no longer ugly. His wounds are now the beauty of paradise. These wounds shine forth more glorious than the sun. These wounds are streams of grace.

For coming to Him in faith, Jesus wants to give you the fullness of these graces. This is why it is far greater that He does not show you, like Thomas the Apostle, His visible wounds. It is because He wants to pour out upon you the invisible graces of these wounds, with all of the merits, the glory, the beauty and the healing love which flows from these wounds.

With each holy hour you make, you are saying to Jesus: "My Lord and my God!" JN 20:28).

And each time He is saying to you: Blessed are you, Thomas, because you have not seen, and yet, have believed.

Fraternally yours in
His Eucharistic Love,

Msgr. Pepe

Msgr. Pepe

THE BEST PART

Feast Day of St. Mary Magdalene
July 22, 1993

J.M.J.

Dear Fr. Thomas,

Yesterday I offered Holy Mass for the Missionaries of Charity. It reminded me of the first time I met Mother Teresa of Calcutta. When she came to Manila to establish a community here, I was asked to offer Mass for her and her sisters.

After Mass I had the privilege of speaking with her in private. That was when she told me the history of her community. Sister Agnus, a little, dark nun from India, was her first follower. There were just a few sisters with Mother Teresa in the beginning, yet there were so many people in need. From the old and sick, dying on the street, to the abandoned babies and children, who had no one to take care of them, Mother Teresa wanted to reach out to all of them.

The question was, how to do it with so few? There was not enough time in the day to take care of all of those in need. Mother and the sisters prayed in order to find out what to do. The answer was surprising. Beside their regular prayers, God wanted something very special. Even though there seemed to be not enough time in the day as it was, God wanted something more. He wanted the community to set aside an extra hour everyday to come together for a holy hour of prayer in the Presence of His Son exposed in the Blessed Sacrament.

Mother Teresa testifies that this daily holy hour is both the cause and the reason why her community has blossomed. Through the power and graces flowing from the daily holy hour, the community has grown to over three thousand. Through these sisters, Mother Teresa has multiplied herself and is now present in every part of the world. Because she was willing to take time to unite herself with the "Vine", she is now able to reach out and embrace the whole world.

At His Last Supper Discourse, Jesus said that whoever remained in union with Him in the Blessed Sacrament will bear much fruit (JN 15:5). The apostolic fruit of Mother Teresa and her sisters continues to amaze the world.

Her story inspired me to do the same thing that she did. I had been reading about the apostolate of perpetual adoration and how Fr. Martin Lucia was promoting this successfully throughout the United States and other countries. I wanted it spread throughout the entire Philippines. This is why I founded the community called The Eucharistic Disciples of St. Pius X. Day and night without pause they go before the Blessed Sacrament in loving adoration. First they prayed that Fr. Martin would come to the Philippines and begin the great apostolate of establishing perpetual adoration in parishes. Then they prayed that it would spread throughout the country. There are now 500 chapels. Now the Eucharistic Disciples pray that we reach our goal of 1000 chapels of perpetual adoration in parishes.

These two examples of Mother Teresa and the Eucharistic Disciples illustrate the truth of what Jesus said in today's gospel: "Martha, Martha, you are anxious and upset about many things. One thing alone is necessary. Mary your sister has chosen the best part and it shall not be taken from her" (LK 10:41, 42).

The best part is being with Jesus in the Blessed Sacrament. The best time you spend on earth, dear Thomas, is time spent with your best friend, Jesus, in the most Blessed Sacrament. And it is the surest way of bearing great apostolic fruit.

Fraternally yours in
His Eucharistic Love,

Msgr. Pepe

Msgr. Pepe

THE BEST HOMILY OF ALL

Feast Day of St. John Vianney
August 4, 1993

J.M.J.

Dear Fr. Thomas,

Do you remember George, a young friend of mine that you met at Binondo Church? He told me that he would like to enter the seminary and become a priest. He said that the only problem was that he would not be able to memorize a homily, nor learn to give so many of them. After thinking about what he said, I told him that I did not think that there was a problem.

The greatest priest who ever lived would give the same homily every time, over and over, and it was just two lines. St. John Vianney would tell the people every Sunday: "If you only knew how much Jesus loves you in the Blessed Sacrament, you would die of happiness." Then pointing to the Tabernacle he would say "JESUS IS REALLY THERE."

People came from all over France to hear him talk; and he would say the same thing every Sunday. So profoundly moved to the very depth of his soul at the realization of the love and presence of Jesus in the Blessed Sacrament, that when he pointed to the Tabernacle to tell the people that Jesus is really there, he would begin to weep for joy. He would spend hours in prayer before the Blessed Sacrament everyday and every night, and hours in the confessional each day hearing confessions. St. John Vianney, the Cure of Ars, was proclaimed by the Church to be the Model and Patron of all priests.

Another famous priest who lived during the time of St. John Vianney was Pere Lacordiere. This priest was the most eloquent speaker of his day. When he spoke at Notre Dame in Paris, the King and Queen would come to hear him and the Cathedral would be filled.

One day, someone asked him if it gave him great satisfaction to be such a popular speaker. He said it did not because when he spoke everyone said how smart and intelligent he was. But when John Vianney spoke everyone said how good Jesus is!!

How complicated human nature is, dear Thomas, We try to impress everyone with how intelligent we are by theologizing everything so much that people find it hard to understand what exactly we are trying to say. What we really have to do is just tell people how good Jesus is in the Blessed Sacrament! I told George that all he has to do as a priest is repeat the two lines of St. John Vianney and he will also be canonized a Saint.

Fraternally yours in
His Eucharistic Love,

Msgr. Pepe

Msgr. Pepe

REAL POWER

Feast of the Transfiguration
August 6, 1993

J.M.J.

Dear Fr. Thomas,

World War II seems long ago and far away. On this day in 1945 two bombs were dropped on Japan. The war ended. At that time there was a young man here in a Japanese concentration camp by the name of Douglas Valentine. Many years later he wrote a book called Hotel Tacloban, a nickname for the camp.

Critical of the American government, the book did not sell very well except in such places as Nigeria. There in the Cathedral at Awka someone must have forgotten and left a copy in the pew. Fr. Martin saw the book when he went into the Cathedral to make a holy hour. Because the title was a city in the Philippines, he opened the book and read one page.

It told about a Filipino deacon who visited Douglas Valentine while he was convalescing on a ship after the liberation. The deacon wanted to leave Valentine with one lasting, happy memory of the Philippines to erase all the bad ones he had in the concentration camp.

With that said the deacon picked up his guitar and sang the Spanish song "You Belong to My Heart." In Spanish it's "Solamente Una Vez." The magnificent words to the song were translated on the next page.

What was the inspiration obtained from the moment? Each one belongs to the Heart of Jesus. Through the power of perpetual adoration, each one will return to His Heart. A community of priests is needed to spread perpetual adoration throughout the world.

Fr. Martin was telling this story to two of the first ones to be ordained for the Missionaries of the Blessed Sacrament. They were sitting in the airport in Cebu waiting for the flight to Tagbilaran. At that precise moment a young man came along with a guitar and asked if he could sing a song. The song he sang was "You Belong to My Heart."

On this anniversary of the dropping of the bomb, should we not think of this? If something man-made can be used with such a destructive force, we have not even begun to see the constructive power of God's uncreated love in the Blessed Sacrament.

Peter, James and John witnessed the Transfiguration of Christ on Mount Tabor. The whole world will witness the glorious transfiguration of Christ in the Blessed Sacrament. It will have the exact opposite effect of the bomb dropped on Nagasaki. At the transfiguration of Christ in the Blessed Sacrament, there will be an explosion of divine energy which will release the power of His love and renew the face of the earth. Then the world will see Real Power! All will be made well. All will belong to His Heart. All will be made one.

In the meantime, there are five graces we receive each time we visit Jesus in the Blessed Sacrament. By His glorious wounds we are the ones who are transfigured and changed through His healing love. Restoration, sanctification, transformation, reparation and salvation are the graces being poured out graciously upon us with each holy hour we make.

Like Peter, dear Thomas, this is why we should exclaim in His Divine Presence, "Lord, how good it is for us to be here!"

Fraternally yours in
His Eucharistic Love,

Msgr. Pepe

Msgr. Pepe

BEGGING FOR LOVE

Feast Day of St. Clare
August 11, 1993

J.M.J.

Dear Fr. Thomas,

In this letter I am enclosing a holy card of St. Clare, whose feast day we celebrate today. Notice that she is holding a monstrance with the Blessed Sacrament. This is how she is always pictured, in cards, statues and stained glass windows.

That St. Clare is always shown with the Blessed Sacrament has a two-fold significance. The first is to express her great love for the Blessed Sacrament. The second is to demonstrate her great faith in the power of the Blessed Sacrament.

When her convent was being attacked she held up the Blessed Sacrament in full view of the vandals and they fled in fright. The Blessed Sacrament saved her community from being destroyed.

When St. Clare first met St. Francis he told her that he did not believe that she was sincere. To prove her love for God she had to go out into the streets begging for bread. Because she came from a very wealthy family, that took as much humility then in the 13th century, as it would today in the 20th century.

Think of the poor beggars who wait at the traffic lights and knock on the window of every passing car. Imagine asking a rich young woman to do this today for the love of God.

Do we have a St. Clare today? I am sure that we do in the person of Sister Briege McKenna. In 1970, Jesus spoke to Sister Briege from the Blessed Sacrament. It was not an interior voice, it was audible. He wanted her to minister to His priests.

Since then, Sister Briege has given hundreds and hundreds of retreats to priests. You may want to read her book, "Miracles Do Happen." She has touched the hearts of thousands of priests, affirming each one in their priesthood. There is not a Bishop anywhere in the world that does not know of the great work she has done for the church. When Sister Briege came to Manila, she said that the two things that the devil hated the most was the priesthood and the Holy Eucharist. Like Saint Clare, Sister Briege spends many hours each day in prayer before the Blessed Sacrament.

With all of the retreats that Sister Briege has given all over the world, one of my favorite stories is a retreat that Sister Briege did not give. She was scheduled to give a retreat to the Bishops of Nigeria. Civil unrest broke out and she could not get a flight to Jos where the Bishops had gathered.

Since Fr. Martin was in the diocese preaching on perpetual adoration, he was asked by Bishop Ganaka to give the retreat instead. One of the Bishops was from Awka. His name is Bishop Albert Obinafuna and he invited Fr. Martin to come to his diocese. There he met a young waiter by the name of Fabian Eke.

Fabian became the first vocation from Africa for the Missionaries of the Blessed Sacrament. He has just finished his studies in theology and should be ordained in a year. After ordination, Fabian will do what St. Clare and the companions of St. Francis did. For the love of God he will beg. But he will not beg for bread to eat. He will beg people to love "The Living Bread come down from heaven". He will go back and spread perpetual adoration throughout Africa.

This is what you should do, dear Thomas. You should beg your people to love Jesus in the Blessed Sacrament. You should have perpetual adoration in your parish. Love humbles itself. And the more one loves, the more one is willing to be humble and beg for the other.

If St. Clare was ashamed to beg, there never would be the Poor Clare Community. There would not be a Sister Briege McKenna touching the hearts of all these priests and bringing them to the Blessed Sacrament as she goes around the world begging for love.

You see, dear Thomas, Sister Briege is a Poor Clare nun who lives in Florida at St. Clare Convent.

Fraternally yours in
His Eucharistic Love,

Msgr. Pepe
Msgr. Pepe

IMITATION

Feast Day of Saint Maximilian Kolbe
August 14, 1993

J.M.J.

Dear Fr. Thomas,

My letter today is about an airplane ride I took from Manila to Cebu. Before we boarded, I saw something that really inspired me. A woman whose name was Angela was wait-listed. She pleaded her case to the clerk. Her father was very ill and she needed to be at his side. But, there was nothing anyone could do. The flight was fully booked and it was a matter of three or four days before Angela could be confirmed.

Then something wonderful happened. A young man stepped up and gave Angela his seat. He was willing to wait for hours, even days, in a hot, uncomfortable airport, in order that Angela could be free to go at once to be with her father.

On the flight to Cebu, I was thinking how unselfish this act was. Then I thought of St. Maximilian Kolbe. How much more inspiring was the unselfish act he performed! He is the priest who gave up his life for a fellow prisoner in the concentration camp of Auschwitz. He was willing to die so that a fellow prisoner with a family could be set free.

Noted for his heroic sacrifice and great missionary work, founder of the Militia Immaculatae Movement, which has millions of consecrants to Mary spread throughout the world, Maximilian Kolbe was one of the first saints canonized by Pope John Paul II.

Some criticized the Holy Father for this because there were no miracles to "prove" that Maximilian Kolbe was a saint. The obvious answer, of course, is that his life was a miracle of unselfishness. This unselfishness is an example to all of us in a day, and an age of self-centeredness. They call this the "me generation".

But what inspired Maximilian Kolbe? It was the Blessed Sacrament, dear Thomas. He spoke to his confreres in the community at Niepokalanow about Jesus in the Blessed Sacrament as "the elder Brother and Bridegroom of souls, present in the Eucharist; He makes us brothers, He warms our hearts with mutual love."

Father Maximilian encouraged adoration of the Blessed Sacrament as "the most important activity". He dreamed that in the chapel of Niepokalanow the Lord Jesus would be exposed in a monstrance day and night. In 1938, he stated: "My aim is to institute perpetual adoration. When we come to the chapel, we gain for ourselves and for others many graces, particularly if the whole day is given to adoration of the Blessed Sacrament. By this adoration a tremendous amount of good is done."

In speaking about perpetual adoration he said: "There flows an uninterrupted stream of prayer. Prayer is the greatest power in the universe, capable of transforming each of us, capable of changing the face of the earth."

In 1920, Father Maximilian made a resolution to visit the Blessed Sacrament thirty times each day. Fr. Pal, a colleague and contemporary testifies that it was easy to find him and know what he was doing because he was always in the chapel in adoration.

This is what inspired Fr. Kolbe to switch with his fellow prisoner. Countless times he had meditated on this truth in the Presence of Our Savior. Jesus chose death on the cross that we may have the fullness of His life in the Blessed Sacrament. He chose hatred that we may be filled with His love. He chose to be wounded beyond recognition that we may be healed to perfection. He chose the darkness of the terrible abyss that we may have the light and joy of His Real Presence. He chose the agony of being totally abandoned by heaven that we may always have Him, Emmanuel, with us on earth.

Fr. Kolbe told his brothers: "All the young brothers must try to imitate the Elder Brother Jesus in the Most Blessed Sacrament."

And this is what Fr. Kolbe did himself when he exchanged his own life for that of his fellow prisoner. The greatest effect of his devotion to the Blessed Sacrament was IMITATION. We may not be called to such a dramatic act of unselfishness, but each day we are called to many small acts of unselfishness that should all be motivated, influenced and empowered by the greatest unselfish act of all, the witness of the unselfish love of Jesus in the Most Blessed Sacrament.

Fraternally yours in
His Eucharistic Love,

Msgr. Pepe

Msgr. Pepe

RESTORATION

Feast Day of St. Pius X
August 21, 1993

J.M.J.

Dear Fr. Thomas,

Thank you for saying Mass for the Sisters at Las Piñas. Something happened in that little chapel five years ago that I want to tell you about.

One evening, I came into the chapel for a visit. There was a holy woman by the name of Hilda Walstrum kneeling in prayer. She was weeping softly and I asked her if there was anything wrong. She explained that her tears were tears of joy.

She had attended Mass and at the elevation, she saw the Sacred Host changed into a Heart inflamed with the light of love bursting forth with luminous rays. One of these rays penetrated her heart. She said that she experienced more love in that single instant than it was possible for anyone to receive if they lived a thousand years.

The same thing happened to Sister Agnes of Akita, Japan. She went into the convent chapel to pray and saw a glorious light coming from the Blessed Sacrament. Filled with divine love, she went right down on the floor. For hours no one could even move her. Twenty years after this experience, the very memory of it will move Sister Agnes to ecstacy.

I spoke for hours with Bishop Ito of Akita. He told me that he was there to witness this glorious light from the Blessed Sacrament. It was on the feast of the Sacred Heart in 1973 and it lasted for three days. This apparition has now been approved by the Church. The first one since Fatima in 1916.

At Fatima, 70,000 people witnessed the miracle of the dancing sun. The sun in the sky is a sign of the Son of God in the Blessed Sacrament. One is the natural source of all power and life, the other is the supernatural source. That is why every monstrance is in the form of a sunburst.

The miracle at Fatima foretells the great Eucharistic Miracle that is coming. What happened at Akita tells us the nature of this miracle. In every place where Jesus is adored in the Blessed Sacrament, the light of His love will burst forth like the dawn for everyone to see.

As soon as there are enough chapels of perpetual adoration to satisfy God's divine justice, He will show the whole world His Divine Mercy by revealing what is concealed, making visible what is hidden, the light of His love in the Blessed Sacrament.

What Sister Agnes saw, the whole world will one day see. It will be the glorious light of His love. It will have the power to penetrate every human heart, no matter how cold, no matter how cruel, and bring every human heart back to the Heart of God. Then, once mankind comes back to God through this Eucharistic Miracle, nature will come back to man. And then we will have a second, a new, and a more glorious earthly paradise.

This is the motto of the great pope and saint we celebrate today: "TO RESTORE ALL THINGS TO CHRIST."

Let his motto inspire you, dear Thomas, to have perpetual adoration in your parish. Restoration is the first grace obtained. Each holy hour advances the day when Jesus will restore all things to Himself. Only when we glorify Him in the Blessed Sacrament with our love, will He manifest the glory of His love to all mankind.

Politically, Socially, Economically, Educationally and Morally we are exhausted. We are beyond human solution. What we need is a divine intervention and this divine intervention will be the great eucharistic miracle.

This is why St. Pius called perpetual adoration "the work of works". And he is called the Eucharistic Pope.

Fraternally yours in
His Eucharistic Love,

Msgr. Pepe

Msgr. Pepe

HIS PRECIOUS BLOOD

Triumph of the Cross
September 14, 1993

J.M.J.

Dear Fr. Thomas,

When Cecilia Chin invited me to give a talk in Kansas, I sat next to a man on the airplane from San Antonio, Texas. He knew that I was a priest because I was wearing a collar. During the flight he showed me something that he thought I would be interested in seeing.

It was a third century bronze coin. He wanted to know how much I thought it was worth. I did not know. I was surprised to find out that it was worth $300. This was because it had the face of Constantine stamped on it.

It did interest me because Pope John XXIII used the name of Constantine as the reason for the second Vatican Council. He said the purpose was to open up the window and let fresh air into the Church and get rid of all of the dust that had accumulated since the time of Constantine.

Holding the coin I was thinking about this when my mind began to think about the talk I had to give in Kansas on the Blessed Sacrament. The Eucharist flows from the Passion of Christ. When we come to the Blessed Sacrament WE COME TO THE CROSS. During our holy hour we lift up to the Eucharistic Heart of Jesus those souls in most need of His mercy.

During our holy hour, those in most need of His mercy are stamped and marked with the Precious Blood of Jesus. This includes those who are to die that day. Stamped with the Precious Blood of Jesus, they are saved.

One night at San Miguel Church I had just finished my holy hour when a taxi drove up at 4 A.M. A woman wanted me to talk with her son. They lived in Parañaque. She had been awakened by a voice telling her to come to the church of San Miguel. She got up just in time. Her son was just about to commit suicide. He is now well and has been doing very fine since his visit to San Miguel.

Another night, Nonette Silla was in the chapel praying from 2 A.M. to 3 A.M., the hour before mine. Three weeks before she had lifted up to the Heart of Jesus a man she knew who was destroying the moral life of many of her girlfriends. Her prayer included this man because she knew that Jesus loved him, too. Her prayer ended with an exclamation point that she wanted Jesus to bring him to the chapel so that she would know for sure that he was converted.

Three weeks later while she was in prayer at the chapel she heard someone sobbing in the back. She turned around and it was him. He explained that for three weeks his mind was confused. What he thought was right now looked like it was wrong. He could not sleep. That night he began to drive around the city. He lived in Makati. When he passed the church of San Miguel he saw the light on in the chapel. The light was inviting, welcoming. He decided to stop and come in. What he met was not condemnation for his sins. Instead, he experienced tender mercy from the Blessed Sacrament. That is why he wept.

When I came at 3 A.M. he told me his story. I heard his confession, gave him absolution, and he has been a daily communicant ever since. Nonette's holy hour gave him something of greater value than the face of Constantine. It stamped his soul with the Precious Blood of Jesus and he could not escape God's mercy and grace.

I did not see the movie "Schindler's List", but a friend told me about one touching scene. Schindler removes a gold pin from his lapel and cries that if he had sold that pin, he could have bought one more life, saved one more life. He weeps. He laments that he could have done more.

If only we knew the value of a holy hour we would never miss a single day without making one, dear Thomas.

The Holy Father says in *Dominicae Cenae* that adoration makes "reparation" for the evils of the world. Because the Cross is infinite in merit, there is no limit to the value of a holy hour. That is why Fr. John Hardon S.J. says that it is absolutely impossible to exaggerate the value of a single holy hour of prayer in the Presence of Jesus in the Blessed Sacrament.

Jesus said:
"And when I am lifted up from the earth, I will draw everyone to Myself." (JN 12:32) With each holy hour we draw down upon the parish and the world the graces He won for us at Calvary. The triumph of the cross is the mercy we obtain from the Blessed Sacrament to stamp each and everyone with the Precious Blood of Jesus.

Fraternally yours in
His Eucharistic Love,

Msgr. Pepe
Msgr. Pepe

SANCTIFICATION

Feast Day of St. Therese of the Child Jesus
October 1st, 1993

J.M.J.

Dear Fr. Thomas,

As I look outside my window now, it is pouring down rain. It would be impossible for anyone to go outside at this time without getting soaking wet.

The rain reminds me of what the church teaches about devotion to the Blessed Sacrament. It's guaranteed successful; absolutely the surest way to sanctification. Pope Paul VI says in *Mysterium Fidei* that the most efficacious way of growing in holiness is time spent with Jesus in the Most Blessed Sacrament.

Jesus Himself said His Heart in the Blessed Sacrament is a fountain flowing with living waters and cried out for everyone to come to Him. (JN 7:38)

Each time we come to Him we are sanctified. Each moment efficaciously deepens our union with Christ.

St. Therese, the Little Flower, is absolute proof of this. She became terribly discouraged because she would fall asleep during her holy hour in the Presence of Jesus in the Blessed Sacrament. Since she had joined the Carmelite Monastery to dedicate herself to prayer and the contemplative life, she was tempted to leave because she thought that she was a total failure.

Then Jesus appeared to her and asked her if she remembered what her father said to her when she was a little girl and would fall asleep in his lap. She answered that her father would say that he enjoyed her just as much asleep on his lap, as when she was awake talking with him.

Then, Jesus said: "And it is the same with me!" She died at the age of twenty-four and is known as the greatest Saint of the 20th century. Even when St. Therese was asleep in the chapel she was growing in holiness! Sanctification is the second grace we receive.

And just as one could not go outside now in the pouring rain without getting wet, neither can one come into the presence of the Blessed Sacrament without getting spiritually wet and growing in the very life and holiness of the Lord Himself. This is why scripture says: "He will come to us like the rain; like spring rain that waters the earth." (HOSEA 6:3)

Fraternally yours in
His Eucharistic Love,

Msgr. Pepe

Msgr. Pepe

TRANSFORMATION

Feast Day of St. Francis of Assisi
October 4, 1993

J.M.J.

Dear Fr. Thomas,

One of the most respected and well known women in the Philippines is Conchitina Bernardo. Recently she became a member of the third order of St. Francis. When Conchitina was studying medicine at the University of Madrid in 1963 she met an American student who returned to the States to become a priest.

Almost 25 years went by before these two friends met again in Manila while he was spreading perpetual adoration during the National Eucharistic Year in 1987. Through the years she had developed a deep devotion to the Blessed Sacrament and wanted to help promote it. There was so much work to do that the priest needed assistance. When Fr. Jonas Romea became available I invited him to come to Manila to live with me at San Miguel. Conchitina graciously sponsored his travel expenses which enabled him to join the apostolate and spread perpetual adoration.

When the Eucharistic year ended, Fr. Jonas went to the States where he did so well that his success encouraged this priest to begin a new community of priests to spread perpetual adoration throughout the world. The community is called Missionaries of the Blessed Sacrament. The priest who met Conchitina long ago is Fr. Martin Lucia. And once again, we have a Philippine-American Connection.

Conchitina is one of countless thousands who have been influenced by St. Francis. But Jesus in the Blessed Sacrament is the one who influenced St. Francis. Often he would pray the entire night before the Blessed Sacrament. His one desire in life was transforming union with Christ. One night in July of 1216 Christ appeared to him in the church of Saint Mary of the Angels as he was in prayer before the Blessed Sacrament.

After his vision Francis cried, "I shall send them all to paradise". He was more convinced than ever of the power of prayer to save souls.

On September 14 a seraph with wings of fire - straight out of Isaiah (6:2) swooped down from heaven on Francis as he was contemplating and imprinted on his flesh the mark of the nails as well as the lance wound in his side. Everyone in the region saw the summit of La Verna enveloped with light, as if the sun had already risen. Brother Leo saw a ball of fire descending on Francis's face when he received the stigmata.

I mention this, dear Thomas, because the Blessed Sacrament is the fire of Divine Love. Like fire which transforms everything to itself, one is transformed from glory to glory and made more into the image and likeness of Christ for each moment that one spends in His Divine Presence.

Remember our conversation about the metamorphoses of a caterpillar into a colorful butterfly? The difference amazes us.

The difference in our soul from one holy hour to another amazes the Saints in heaven and the Angels on earth. There is a transformation which takes place in your soul which is more real and dramatic than the transformation which took place in the body of Francis when he received the stigmata. With each passing moment in His Presence, not just your hands and side, but rather, your whole being is being transformed more and more into the very image and likeness of Christ himself.

Because of this transformation, each moment you spend with Jesus on earth will make your soul everlastingly more glorious and beautiful in heaven. This is why St. Paul exclaims, dear Thomas: "All of us gazing upon the Lord are being transformed from glory to glory and being made into his very image and likeness." (2 Cor. 3:18)

Fraternally yours in
His Eucharistic Love,

Msgr. Pepe

Msgr. Pepe

CONNECTIONS

Feast Day of the Holy Rosary
October 7, 1993

J.M.J.

Dear Fr. Thomas,

As you read this letter, please take your rosary out of your pocket and notice how each bead is connected to another. The Blessed Mother does this kind of "connection" with people too. She brings about a chain of events resulting in glory for her Son in the Blessed Sacrament.

For example, exactly four years ago the Holy Father came to Seoul, Korea for the occasion of the 44th International Eucharistic Congress. Much to the encouragement of countless of thousands of people all over the world, the Pope chose to visit a chapel of perpetual adoration as his first stop coming from the airport.

There at the Church of the Good Shepherd, he gave a talk on the importance of adoration in the life of the priest to the Cardinals, Bishops, priests and religious. The Pope said in his talk that it was "most appropriate" that his first visit in Korea be to a church with perpetual adoration.

That evening the executive secretary for the Congress visited Fr. Farrall, Fr. Martin and myself at the Maryknoll house where we were staying. He wanted to know how all of the wonderful work of perpetual adoration came about, with hundreds of chapels in both Korea and the Philippines.

From this meeting with the executive secretary came an invitation to come to Rome to present the Holy Father with an album of all of these chapels in Asia.

Fr. Martin did not want to go unless I joined him. Because it was so important I decided to do so. A date was set and, because we were all coming from different directions, we decided to meet at the chapel of adoration in St. Peter's Basilica at a specific time.

At this happy reunion we met a theology student as we were leaving the chapel at St. Peter's. When he found out why we were in Rome, he said that he wanted to become a priest and spread perpetual adoration, too.

The student is now a priest, Fr. Vincent Perricone, who is spreading perpetual adoration throughout the United Kingdom. Before he left for Manila, he told a lay friend who told Joseph De Luca. Joseph was ordained with Vincent and is now most successful in spreading perpetual adoration throughout the United States. Fr. Joseph has also attracted many other vocations to the Missionaries of the Blessed Sacrament.

Do you now see what I mean about "connections", Thomas? From Seoul to Rome to Manila to all over the world, the Blessed Mother is making a "living rosary" to glorify her Son in the Blessed Sacrament.

If you are still holding your rosary, there is just one more thing that I want to say about it. When you pray the Rosary in the presence of the Blessed Sacrament, you love Jesus with the Heart of Mary. United to the Heart of Mary through the rosary you make a perfect holy hour because you love Jesus with the perfect love of Mary.

Fraternally yours in
His Eucharistic Love,

Msgr. Pepe

Msgr. Pepe

REPARATION

Feast Day of St. Margaret Mary
October 16, 1993

J.M.J.

Dear Fr. Thomas,

If you get a chance to see the play "Les Miserables," please do so. I liked it better than "Miss Saigon." Please don't miss it. You know that Lea Salonga is in it and she is terrific. But, more importantly, this Victor Hugo classic has a message that screams out to be heard today.

Valjean is a poor carpenter without any work. His crime: stealing a loaf of bread to feed some starving children. His sentence: five years in prison. He tries to escape and is recaptured to serve the state's cruel justice of fifteen more years. There in prison he is forgotten and abandoned by his own.

Could this not be the story of Jesus in the Blessed Sacrament? To feed the spiritually starved children of His Father, Jesus becomes the Living Bread come down from Heaven. This is His "crime." He is not rewarded with thanksgiving and adoration. He is punished by being thrown into the prison of the Tabernacle. There in the dungeon He is forgotten and abandoned by his own. Ashamed, we do not expose Him. Too busy, we do not honor Him. The monstrance is His throne where He wants to be set free and reign as King of Love. Instead, He is shut up and treated like the criminal Valjean.

He describes Himself as a Prisoner of Love.

Dear Thomas, there is no exaggeration in any of what I say. All of this is what Jesus Himself revealed to St. Margaret Mary. She was in prayer when He appeared to her from the Blessed Sacrament and said: "Behold this Heart which loves so much and, yet, is so little loved in return." He explained that the thorns around His Heart are symbolic of the pain that He suffers because of the ingratitude and indifference of His priests and people toward His love in the Blessed Sacrament. Then, Jesus said that He suffers more now because of this indifference and ingratitude than He did during His entire passion.

For this reason Jesus makes this appeal to each of us: "I thirst with such a terrible thirst to be loved by you in this Most Blessed Sacrament."

The Blessed Sacrament is the Sacred Heart of Jesus in our midst. Today He weeps as He wept over Jerusalem. How He longs to gather each one to Himself as a mother hen gathers her little chicks. Change His weeping to a smile, dear Thomas.

Have perpetual adoration in your parish and you will change the thorns in His Heart to many flowers of consolation. Each holy hour will make reparation for all of the indifference and ingratitude of the world. What a grace!

Fraternally yours in
His Eucharistic Love,

Msgr. Pepe

Msgr. Pepe

SALVATION

Feast Day of St. Martin de Porres
November 3rd, 1993

J.M.J.

Dear Fr. Thomas

I was reading the newspaper this morning about a man from Thailand who should win the Nobel Peace Award for his humanitarian service. Each weekend he comes down from his mountain village and goes into Bangkok. There he searches for young girls who were abducted, kidnapped or tricked and brought to one of the many of hundreds of brothels in the city.

These girls are between the ages of twelve and fourteen and have as many as ten customers a night. This man travels a long distance, gets no pay, and risks his life to save them. He has succeeded in bringing over 400 back to their parents and family. Imagine the joy of a father or mother in seeing their little girl coming back safely to them after such a terrible ordeal? Think of how grateful the parents must be to this man for saving their little girl.

That is nothing in comparison to how grateful God the Father would be to you for having perpetual adoration in your parish, dear Thomas. This is why our Holy Father, Pope John Paul II, beatified Dina Belanger.

She was a Canadian woman devoted to prayer before the Blessed Sacrament. Before her holy hour Jesus would show her multitudes of souls on the precipice of hell. She would see these same souls in the hands of God after her holy hour.

Jesus gave Blessed Dina a message to give to the church. The value of a holy hour is so great that it brings multitudes of souls from the edge and brink of hell to the very gates of heaven.

Think of it this way, Thomas. Because St. Martin was black and illegitimate he was insulted and mistreated. He identified with Jesus, ignored and mistreated in the Blessed Sacrament. As they consoled each other, Martin became more charitable, not hostile, better not bitter. He would spend as many as eight hours each day in prayer before the Blessed Sacrament.

This so pleased Jesus that he made Martin a miracle worker. He would take a basket of fresh bread from the monastery and go out into the streets to feed the poor. With a single basket of bread he would feed an entire barrio.

Martin fed hundreds of starving people with a single basket of bread. You, dear Thomas, save hundreds of people from hell with a single holy hour of prayer in the Presence of the Living Bread come down from Heaven.

This is why Charles de Foucauld spent his whole life before the Blessed Sacrament in a desert in Arabia. His one prayer: "My God, bring all men to salvation."

Have perpetual adoration in your parish, dear Father, and God will be infinitely more grateful to you than the parents in Thailand are to the man who saves their little girls from the brothels. God will spend all eternity thanking you for the countless souls you save.

What could be a greater reason for having perpetual adoration than this fifth grace of salvation?

Fraternally yours in
His Eucharistic Love,

Msgr. Pepe

Msgr. Pepe

INTIMACY

Christmas
December 25, 1993

J.M.J.

Dear Father Thomas,

Merry Christmas! A holy night, a silent night, with Mother and child, all is calm, all is bright. This inspiring hymn came to us because an organ in Germany broke down about one hundred years ago.

Without an organ the parish priest in this small country church said it would be a "Silent Night". The organist would compose a melody. The priest would write the lyrics and the choir would just sing the soft praises of this hymn for midnight Mass.

That is all it was meant to be, just a simple hymn sung once and forgotten. Then a snowstorm prevented the man who fixed the organ from coming until the snow melted in the spring. After he finished he noticed the music left on the organ since Christmas night and took it back to Munich. The rest is history. "Silent Night" has reverberated throughout the ages. With its quiet sounds of love and peace it has inspired millions and millions, touching the lives of countless people.

It is the same with a holy hour. We leave it in the chapel like the music to "Silent Night," and God turns our hour of prayer into a never-ending stream of graces for His people. A single holy hour of prayer touches more hearts through God's grace, than all the people who have been touched by "Silent Night". From a single holy hour of prayer God's graces reverberate throughout the world until the end of time and will continue for all eternity.

This is because of the divine appreciation God has for those who love His Son in the Blessed Sacrament. The Father will spend all eternity thanking you and loving you in heaven because you have honored His Son on earth in the Blessed Sacrament. The Blessed Sacrament is the continuation of Christ's Incarnation on earth.

Coming to the Blessed Sacrament we find the same humility and gentleness that the shepherds found in "the babe lying in a manger". (LUKE 2:16) The hunger in the heart of God for the love of man is expressed in the profound humility of these two words, Baby Jesus.

How great is God's desire for intimacy with man! Jesus came as a Babe, because no one is ever afraid to come close to a baby. A baby is lovable in its vulnerability. A baby reaching out for love with open arms is irresistible.

The Sacred Host embodies the Divine Tenderness of the Incarnation. So gentle and humble, so loving and so small and vulnerable, the Blessed Sacrament is Jesus saying "Come to Me ... for I am gentle and humble of Heart". (Mt 11:28, 29)

Only the humble hear His voice. Only those with a childlike heart seek His Heart in the Blessed Sacrament. This is why Jesus says: "Let the little children come to Me; do not prevent them for the Kingdom of God belongs to such as these." (Mk 10:14)

The apostles were discouraging the little children from going to Jesus then, just as now some priests discourage people from going to the Blessed Sacrament, exposition or perpetual adoration. It reminds me of a movie called "Golden Child." The child is destined to save the world because everything he touches is healed and made perfect. The devil locks the child in a cage and keeps the child away from the people. The mission is to free the child.

St. Joseph had to protect the Christ Child by the flight into Egypt. A furious Herod ordered a massacre. (Mt 2:16) The Pope likens this to the abortion of human life. There is also the abortion of divine life. Those who destroy adoration cut off the faithful from the flow of divine life.

Reflecting on the writings of Bishop Manuel Gonzales at the Eucharistic Congress in Seville, Spain, the Holy Father called for perpetual adoration in every parish throughout the world. Bishop Gonzales inspired Bishop Felix Zafra. Bishop Zafra inspired the Missionaries of the Blessed Sacrament.

Bishop Gonzales likens coming to the Blessed Sacrament to coming into the warm light of the sun, drinking from the life-giving waters of a refreshing spring, and being absorbed by the sweet fragrance of a flower. But they are not sad if we do not come, because the sun, the fountain and the flower do not have a heart.

The Heart of Jesus is sad if we do not come to Him, because His Heart is the most sensitive and tenderest of all hearts. "Yet, though I stooped to feed My child they did not know that I was their Healer." (Hosea 11:4)

Like the star over Bethlehem, the Pope has put the spotlight on the Blessed Sacrament as the "Healer" of all of our ills, both in the church and in the world. The solution to all of the confusion and promiscuity in the world is intimacy with Jesus in the Blessed Sacrament. To avoid His call to intimacy is the cause of all promiscuity.

Tonight at midnight Mass, "Just a Closer Walk with Thee" was sung by Joseph Skelton, Keith Poupard, George Wilson and Lou Verroi. It is as simple as that. The continuation of Christ's Incarnation in the Blessed Sacrament is Jesus himself coming intimately close to us so that we may come intimately close to Him!

"'Amen, I say to you, whoever does not accept the Kingdom of God like a child will not enter it.' Then He embraced them and blessed them, placing His hands on them." (Mk 10: 15, 16)

That is perpetual adoration, Thomas. The Blessed Sacrament is Emmanuel, "God with us," who has "stooped" with infinite humility and love so that He may continue to embrace, bless and heal all of His children today, just as He did in the gospel then.

The Church was never meant to be so excessively institutional, bureaucratic or legalistic, but rather warm, personal and intimate. People are attracted to what is friendly and loving. Perpetual adoration is Jesus saying to His people "Mi casa es tu casa." A closed door shuts people out and is a sign of that institutionalism that everyone finds distasteful.

Perpetual adoration is a door always open. It is a sign of the open arms of Christ in the Blessed Sacrament always inviting, welcoming and embracing each one who comes to Him. A door always open with the waiting, open arms of Christ, gives everyone a sense of belonging. A door always open exposing the light of Divine Love in the monstrance defines the true meaning of the Incarnation. In the Blessed Sacrament the Word continues to become flesh and dwell among us. Just as the Babe lying in the manger, we can see in the Sacred Host the same "glory of an Only Son, coming from the Father, filled with enduring love." (Jn 1:14)

This is why Mother Teresa says when we look at the Sacred Host we see how much Jesus loves us NOW. This enduring love is His eternal love for you. This enduring love moves you to "Cast all of your worries upon Him because He cares for you." (1 Pt 5:7)

In total trust, surrender all your fears and anxieties to His Heart in exchange for His peace. The only sound He wants you to hear in your head and heart is the sound of this enduring love. Each holy hour should be like the song: "There is a kind of hush all over the world tonight. So listen very carefully, closer now and you will see what I mean. It isn't a dream. The only sound that you will hear is when I whisper in your ear, I LOVE YOU forever and ever."

This enduring love of Jesus in the Blessed Sacrament is why we can still say silent night, holy night, all is calm, all is bright. Sleep in heavenly peace.

This enduring love is why we should be as excited about having a chapel of perpetual adoration as the angel proclaiming the good news of His coming in Bethlehem, the first chapel of perpetual adoration. Be that angel, that messenger, dear Thomas, and tell the people with the same excitement that your parish will have perpetual adoration where the same Jesus born in Bethlehem will be waiting for you with open arms. "You have nothing to fear! I come to proclaim good news for you ... tidings of great joy to be shared by the whole people." (Lk 2: 10)

Fraternally yours in
His Eucharistic Love,

Msgr. Pepe
Msgr. Pepe

SECURITY

St. John the Apostle
December 27, 1993

J.M.J.

Dear Fr. Thomas,

On a cold, winter day in New England two friends of mine, Bruce and Maureen Smith, were driving me to the airport. We kept looking out the window and wondering if the plane was going to be able to take off. It was a dark, gray, cloudy day and so cold it was raining ice.

The plane did take off and within seconds rose above the clouds. The scene was breathtaking. As far as the eye could see, there were rows and rows of white undulating clouds tinged with the brightness of a golden sun.

This, I thought, is what each holy hour should be. "I am the Light of the World." (Jn 8:12) Jesus is the Light. The Blessed Sacrament is Jesus. The Blessed Sacrament is the Light of the World. Negative and discouraging thoughts do not come from Him, but from His adversary.

Each moment in His Presence should influence and move our mind from the negative to the positive. Love is positive. God is Love. (1 Jn 4:8) Jesus is God. Therefore the Blessed Sacrament is Love. The power of this love is transcending. Like the airplane, it takes us from dark, cold, and cloudy thinking to the warm, clear light of positive love.

How often we hear people say that this or that person is "insecure." We are all insecure. We find our security in the depth of His Eucharistic Love. This is the lesson of today's feast. St. John saw himself as "the one whom Jesus loved" and leaned on His Heart. At the first Eucharist John "was reclining at Jesus' side." (Jn 13:23)

This is how we become secure, leaning on the Heart of Christ. When we "lean" on ourselves, we see ourselves in the darkness of our fallen human nature and are consequently "insecure."

Leaning on the Heart of Christ, is seeing ourselves in the light of His Eucharistic Love. A single drop of water has every right to feel insecure. That same drop of water placed in a chalice of wine which becomes the Precious Blood of Jesus has infinite value.

Apart from His love, we are nothing and should feel insecure. United to His Heart we have the infinite value of the drop of water becoming wine which is changed into the Precious Blood. Pride focuses on who we are apart from Christ. Humility shows us our infinite value in Christ, redeemed in His Blood, covered with His love. Then we are most secure!

Jesus did not love John more. John was just more open to the personal love Jesus had for him. This is why he saw himself as "the one whom Jesus loved." He knew, was open to, and appreciated this personal love of Jesus. This is what Our Holy Father tells us we must do in *Redeemer of Man*.

He says that our personal love for Jesus in the Blessed Sacrament must go together with our communal love for Jesus at Mass in order that our love may be complete. Pope John Paul II goes on to say that "our essential commitment in life is to grow spiritually in the climate of the Holy Eucharist."

Just as one can't be exposed to the sun without receiving its rays, neither can one come into the Presence of Jesus in the Blessed Sacrament without receiving His Divine rays and growing spiritually in the light of His love. A holy hour is leaning on the Heart of Jesus. It is a lesson from the Master that each one is "the one whom Jesus loves."

For this reason, every Catholic should shout out to every evangelical and fundamentalist: "I have a personal relationship with Jesus, my Savior!"

How can one develop a personal relationship with someone who is not there? The Blessed Sacrament is Jesus there in Person. "If anyone would serve Me, let him follow Me; where I am, there will My servant be." (Jn 12:26)

There is a long line of great servants with the name John who, like the Beloved Apostle, follow Him where He is in the most Blessed Sacrament.

Pope John XXIII in his autobiography Journal of a Soul... stated that his aim was frequent visits to the Blessed Sacrament where he found his security. This made him the jolly Pope that the world came to love.

Pope John Paul I... found his security in the Presence of the Blessed Sacrament where he preferred to be, in contrast to receiving all of the applause and praise of the world. When asked why he smiled so much, he answered: "Because Jesus in the Blessed Sacrament loves me so much."

Pope John Paul II makes two holy hours of prayer each day and according to a cardinal close to him, makes at least twenty visits to the Blessed Sacrament each day.

Bishop John Magee of Clone, Ireland... the only man in history who has been secretary to three Popes. This saintly bishop has established perpetual adoration in most of the parishes of his diocese where vocations have tripled over the past three years. His brother Cahil Magee promotes perpetual adoration throughout Ireland where there are over one hundred parishes with perpetual adoration.

Saint John Neumann... presented the idea of forty hours devotion to the priests of Philadelphia. The idea was rejected because it was thought to be too dangerous due to the "know-nothings," a group of men who terrorized any immigrant from Europe. The night hours were the ones thought to be too dangerous.

A week after the presentation a fire broke out in the Bishop's house. His office was burned to the ground with everything in it, except for a couple of pieces of paper on the floor untouched by the fire.

The Bishop looked in amazement. They were his plans for forty hours devotion. Then Jesus spoke to him: "If I can save a couple of pieces of worthless paper from a raging fire, how much more will I protect my people coming to adore Me in the Blessed Sacrament." As soon as forty hours devotion began, the "know-nothings" disbanded.

Fr. John Randell received the same message from the Lord while in a holy hour before the Blessed Sacrament. He opened the Bible up to Haggai and Zechariah and received this word. "When you become zealous for my glory in the sanctuary, then I will make the streets safe for the people." Fr. John took "zealous" to mean perpetual adoration. He was in a crime infested area in downtown Providence, Rhode Island. People were moving out of the parish because the area was not safe. The Bishop was thinking about closing the parish when Fr. John got this message. Now it is a thriving parish and the neighborhood has been made safe through perpetual adoration.

Fr. John's testimony inspired Bishop Profugio of Lucena to do the same. He has given witness that perpetual adoration saved his diocese from communism which threatened to tear it apart.

John Mackenzie... first thing he does each morning when he wakes up is to thank Jesus for the personal love He has for him in the Blessed Sacrament and for calling him to Manila to study for the Missionaries of the Blessed Sacrament.

Fraternally yours in
His Eucharistic Love,

Msgr. Pepe

Msgr. Pepe

IN THE PRESENCE OF GREATNESS

Feast Day of St. Thomas Aquinas
January 28, 1994

J.M.J.

Dear Father Thomas,

How I love this Saint Thomas Aquinas! He was as big in body as he was great in spirit. In other words, he was pretty fat! Some say that I am the Santa Claus of the Philippines. I really don't know if this is because of my smile, my laugh, or my weight. In any case, if I am the Santa Claus of the Philippines, then Saint Thomas was the Santa Claus of Italy.

Historians say that workman had to cut out a portion of the table so Thomas could fit. He was so big he had a difficult time sitting down to eat because there was not enough room between the table and the bench. Anyway, he should be the patron of all of us who are on a diet and trying to lose weight.

Some ask what St. Thomas would say if he would come back and visit our seminaries. He is the greatest mind in the history of the church. For centuries his scholastic theology and philosophy was taught in all our seminaries. Now his name is not even mentioned.

If he came back I don't think he would care that he has been forgotten. St. Thomas himself said it best a long time ago. He said before he died that he got more out of a holy hour of prayer before the Blessed Sacrament than all of the books he ever read. He said that he learned more about Jesus in one holy hour than all he ever heard or read. He discovered more about His love being in His Real Presence, than all he ever wrote. And all that has ever been written and said was as meaningless as straw, in comparison to the meaningfulness of a single personal encounter with Jesus in the Blessed Sacrament.

Theology is the study about God. Prayer before the Blessed Sacrament gives us knowledge of God Himself. One is the academic study of love, the other is the warm experience of Love Personified. One may be likened to a book all about a person, while the other is that Person telling us first hand all about Himself.

There is one university in Houston, Texas that teaches Thomistic philosophy and theology. It's run by the Basilian fathers and is called St. Thomas University. There is also in Texas a very famous man who is a legend in golf and played in the 30's, 40's and 50's. Some say that he is the greatest golfer who ever lived. His name is Ben Hogan.

One night coming back from a golf tournament, Ben Hogan had a terrible automobile accident. He hit another car "head on". He almost died. The doctors said that he would never walk again. Through sheer determination, he not only learned to walk again, but went on to win four U.S. opens and another three major tournaments.

I have an American friend who grew up in Texas. Since he was a teenager in the 50's, he has been playing golf. Ben Hogan was his hero. All his life he read every book ever printed on Ben Hogan, everything about his life, his times, and all of his instructional material.

Then one day it finally happened. This friend of mine was in Fort Worth, Texas on a business trip and was invited to lunch at the Colonial Country Club. There he got to meet Ben Hogan in person!

This was in June of 1991. Almost forty years had passed by since my friend first heard of Ben Hogan. Now here he was sitting with the "Master" himself, listening to every word, totally awed in being in the presence of greatness.

My friend could hardly wait to tell all of his friends, as well as all of those who were not his friends. It did not matter. Anyone who he talked to he was just bursting with excitement to tell them that he met Ben Hogan. Friends or strangers, it did not matter. He told them that for forty five minutes he talked with Ben Hogan in person.

Should we not be just as excited at being able to be with Jesus Himself in the Blessed Sacrament? Think about it, Thomas. Was this not what the Angelic Doctor was talking about. My friend had read and heard everything about Ben Hogan, but it could not compare to a single moment of being in his company.

Should we not also be totally awed in being in the presence of greatness for each single moment we spend in the presence of the Blessed Sacrament? He is the Teacher, the Master, the Creator of the entire Universe.

St. Thomas treats in his theology why it is that appreciation for the Holy Eucharist diminishes and why we take for granted the presence of Jesus in the Blessed Sacrament. The scholarly saint speaks of the inseparable relationship between consuming and adoring, between communion of the Holy Eucharist and adoration of the Blessed Sacrament. He says that unless we adore what we consume we lose sight and appreciation of what we are consuming.

In other words, the Eucharist is not a thing but a person. Unless we are willing to take time out and develop a personal relationship with Jesus in the Blessed Sacrament, we lose sight of the lovable person of Jesus in the Blessed Sacrament and the Holy Eucharist diminishes in value in our sight.

St Thomas spent hour after hour in profound adoration of the Blessed Sacrament. Because of his love for the Blessed Sacrament he is called the Angelic Doctor. His love for Jesus in the Eucharist inspired all of the Benediction Hymns like "Tantum Ergo."

The theme of these hymns is the ability of the light of our faith to transcend the senses and grasp the reality of God's presence in the Blessed Sacrament.

Santo Thomas is where I studied philosophy and theology. For this reason, St. Thomas is one of my patron saints.

Let us pray, dear Thomas, that every priest will be imbued with the same love for the Holy Eucharist as St. Thomas Aquinas. As a matter of fact, would that every priest would be as excited about the Blessed Sacrament, Jesus with us in Person, as my friend in Texas was when he met Ben Hogan in person. We could convert the entire world to Catholicism by bursting with excitement in telling everyone that Jesus is really here in Person!

Fraternally yours in
His Eucharistic Love,

Msgr. Pepe

Msgr. Pepe

EUCHARISTIC VISION

St. John Bosco
January 31, 1994

J.M.J.

Dear Fr. Thomas,

Thank you for all that you do for the youth. Please express my gratitude to the entire ALAGAD NI MARIA community for their dedication to the youth.

The Pope's coming to the Philippines next year should be a tremendous help to your ministry. When he came to Korea he told the youth that they would find their identity in the Eucharist.

The Blessed Sacrament is like a mirror. Looking at the Sacred Host we see the neverending love Christ has for us. This is why John Bosco brought the youth to the Blessed Sacrament and is the champion for the youth. He taught young Dominic to love the Blessed Sacrament and Dominic became a saint too.

What the youth need to know is that Jesus is the easiest person to be with. He is absolutely the easiest person in the world to please.

The great Bishop Sheen was going through a dry period where prayer was so difficult that he would just sit in the chapel without saying a word to Jesus. Because the Bishop did not think his holy hours were pleasing to Jesus, he became discouraged.

Then the Bishop remembered something. His little dog couldn't talk, either. When the Bishop would sit down in his easy chair to read the newspaper, his dog would just sit on the floor next to him and keep him company. Just being there with him, the dog was a great consolation to the Bishop and made him very happy.

As the Bishop was thinking about this, he received an inspiration from God. Bishop Sheen was a great consolation and most pleasing to the Lord by just being there with him in the Blessed Sacrament, even though, like his little dog, he didn't say anything to Jesus while he was there.

I love this story, Thomas, because as you know, I have a little dog, too. And because he is such a great consolation to me I call him "Amigo". I love the story also because something similar happened to a priest friend of mine when I was pastor at San Miguel's.

He was making a holy hour in our chapel of perpetual adoration. It was a terribly hot day and he was so tired and bothered by the heat that he could not pray. Just staying in the chapel for his hour was an effort. He was wondering if his hour had any value when, at that moment, a little white kitten came in.

It was so hot someone left the door open. At first my friend thought how much he hates cats. Then he watched as the little kitten went along each pew until it reached the back where my friend was sitting. The kitten stopped, looked up at my friend, put its head on his shoe like a pillow, and went to sleep.

My friend was thrilled. The little kitten had chosen to rest his head on his shoe. Then my friend heard this inspiration as loud as the Sunday Church Bells. If he who hates cats is so delighted by one choosing to be with him, how much more is Jesus delighted by us, whom he loves infinitely, when we choose to be with Him.

My friend, like Bishop Sheen, was never discouraged again in feeling unable to pray. The mere fact that he was there is a prayer of faith that he really believes that Jesus is there. It is a prayer of love because one chooses to be with those one wants to be with, those one truly loves.

Because you are the most important person in the world to Jesus, He stays day and night in the Blessed Sacrament for love of you. All He is asking is for you, dear Thomas, to find just one hour each day to be with Him.

The main point of every retreat and homily that Bishop Sheen ever gave was an effort to inspire everyone to make a daily holy hour. Before he died he was interviewed on T.V. The question he was asked was who inspired and influenced him? Was it a Pope, a Cardinal, a Bishop, a Priest, or perhaps a Nun?

Bishop Sheen said No. The one who inspired him to make a daily holy hour was a youth. When the Communists took over China they went to one church and locked up the priest in his own house. That became his jail. Then they went to the church, broke into the Tabernacle, threw the Sacred Hosts on the floor and left.

They did not see a young girl kneeling in prayer. She was too small to notice. That night she came back, quietly sneaking past the guards at the priest house, before entering the dark cold church.

There she knelt in a holy hour of prayer before going into the sanctuary to receive her Lord and her God in Holy Communion. At that time Communion was still on the tongue and once a day was all that was allowed.

For this reason the little girl came back every night until all of the sacred hosts were consumed. She bent down to the floor and received Jesus on her tongue. All of this was witnessed by the parish priest from his window, as he saw the little girl in the moonlight.

The priest knew exactly how many hosts were in the ciborium because it was he who counted them and consecrated them. When the last host was consumed on the thirty-sixth night the little girl was discovered by the guards as she was leaving. They grabbed her and beat her to death.

The priest lived to tell the story. When Bishop Sheen heard it as a Seminarian, he made a promise to God to make a holy hour everyday during his entire priestly life, a promise he kept until he died at the age of eighty-two. By then he had inspired countless Bishops and priests to do the same. Few know it was a young person who inspired him.

I tell this story, Thomas, because idealism is the virtue of the young at heart. You have dedicated your priesthood to bringing the youth of the world to Christ. I would only want to add: Christ in the Blessed Sacrament.

This is what Frank Feain has done so successfully in Australia with the community Holy Spirit of Freedom. A young Englishman is trying to do the same thing there. This is what the Holy Father wants.

This is the dream and vision of St. John Bosco. The church was a ship about to sink. Enemies on all sides were trying to destroy it. The Pope guides the church between the two pillars rising from the sea. One pillar was the Blessed Mother, the other was the Blessed Sacrament in the monstrance.

Peace was restored and this ship came into a harbor too magnificent for words to describe. John Bosco thought it was heaven. The Blessed Mother told him it was earth, renewed and transformed through the Eucharistic reign of her Son.

Fraternally yours in
His Eucharistic Love,

Msgr. Pepe
Msgr. Pepe

FOR SOMEONE SPECIAL

St. Valentine's Day
February 14, 1994

J.M.J.

Dear Fr. Thomas,

During my holy hour today, I noticed something unusual, a box of chocolates on the altar. I thought that someone had forgotten and left it there, until I read the card on the box. It read: "To Jesus from Ninay because your love is the sweetest love of all."

Once Ninay was so caught up in the love of Jesus that she made this fervent prayer. Her husband was fetching her after one hour, but Ninay prayed to Jesus to make it possible for her to stay longer in the chapel. His car would not start and by the time it was fixed our dear friend Ninay had six additional hours with the Lord.

One prayer that God the Father cannot refuse is when we pray to be able to love His Son, Jesus, more in the Blessed Sacrament. Love is sweet because it makes one feel very special. The quality of love is that it does, indeed, make one special. This is why the love of Jesus in the Blessed Sacrament is the greatest and sweetest love our hearts will ever know.

His love makes you the most special and important person in the world. God has many individual attributes. Each person represents a special, unique attribute of God, never before created, and never again to be reproduced. God sees Himself in us. In each of us, God sees this special unique quality and attribute that we alone possess. And He would do for you alone what He did for the whole human race. If it meant your salvation, Jesus would do everything all over again just for you.

That is how special you are to Him. But you will never know it unless you know Him in the Blessed Sacrament. The Blessed Sacrament is God's Divine Valentine telling us how infinitely special we are to Him. God did not send candy or a paper valentine, but His only Son.

"Yes, God so loved the World that He gave His only Son... not to condemn... but that the world might be saved through Him." (JN 3:16, 17) Through the Blessed Sacrament, God so loves the world that He continues to send us His only Son, who tells us that the Father loves us as much as He loves the Son. (JN 17:23) In other words, each of us are as special to the Father as Jesus Himself. What sweet love!

This is why the introduction for the feast of the Body and Blood of Christ exclaims: "I will feed you with the best of wheat and with honey from the rock I will fill you." (PS 80:17) Honey flowing from the "Rock" is the sweet divine love of Jesus flowing from His Heart in the Blessed Sacrament. Only a broken heart can taste this sweetness. Only a humble heart can know it. Only a child's heart can love it.

This is why God allows suffering in our life. Like medicine it cures us from the illness of pride. Only when our heart has been broken, or crushed, or defeated, or humiliated or is suffering in anyway, can we experience the full sweetness of His love. For He is the Most Broken One of all.

A lance struck Jesus on the cross that from His Broken Heart may flow the sweetness of His Divine Love to all who come to Him in the Blessed Sacrament. This is why we proclaim at every Benediction: "You have given them Bread from Heaven... Having all sweetness within it."

When I was in Mexico, I saw some children playing a game called "piñata." Blindfolded, the children keep striking an object filled with candy until it breaks open pouring out all of the sweets for the children to eat to their hearts content.

To the broken Heart of Jesus in the Blessed Sacrament come the broken-hearted of the world. The sweetness of His love is balm and consolation for the bitterness of life and all of its painful rejections.

For "the Lord is close to the broken-hearted; and those who are crushed in spirit He saves." (PS 34:19)

This may be why third world countries embrace perpetual adoration more enthusiastically than affluent nations. Fr. Lorenzo Guerrero S.J. had a dream of the Philippines seen at night from far above the earth. The view was magnificent with tiny lights in the center of little hearts lighting up the entire Island. He was told in the dream that these luminous lights were graces coming from the many chapels of perpetual adoration.

When Fr. Martin arrived it was right before the EDSA revolution in 1986. Howard Dee took him to Josephine's Seafood Restaurant at Roxas Blvd. A great friend of Cardinal Sin's, with a deep love for the Eucharist and interest in perpetual adoration. Howard was one of the main reasons why Fr. Martin was invited. In the foyer at the restaurant were decorations for Valentine's Day, one thousand little hearts with tiny electric lights in the center. Fr. Martin said this is how many chapels of perpetual adoration Our Lady wants in the Philippines. Because the Philippines is so special to her Heart and the Heart of her Son she wants one thousand chapels of perpetual adoration. Fr. Roger Cortez is working hard to achieve this goal.

There was a song that said: "What the world needs now is love sweet love." A Pope said: "The Blessed Sacrament is the Living Heart of each of our parishes." (Paul VI *Credo of the People of God*). When I think of the Church and the world today I think we are having a spiritual power shortage, some call it a black out, we call it brown out. "The light came into the world, but men loved darkness rather than light." (JN 3:19)

We must return to the Living Source of Sweet Love, the Divine Valentine, generating the true light whereby we see how special we are. When one feels like dirt one treats others like dirt. When one knows how infinitely special one is, one treats everybody else as special too. The more lovable we see ourselves to be in the light of Eucharistic Love, the more loving we will be with each other.

The Blessed Sacrament is for someone very special. You! The lyrics of the song "So rare" would not begin to compare with how special you are to Him. Jesus is more in love with you than all the love that ever existed in the world since the beginning of time. His very Presence says, "Let me call you sweetheart for I am in love with you. Let me hear you whisper that you love me too." About the Blessed Sacrament it is written: "To fall in love with God is the greatest of all romances. To seek Him, the greatest adventure. To find Him, the greatest human achievement."

This morning Vice-President Salvador Laurel came to the opening of the chapel on Carnation St. He is a real hero of the EDSA revolution and considered by many to be one of the greatest statesmen of the 20th century. He told the Missionaries of the Blessed Sacrament that we need another revolution; one to bring the whole world to the Blessed Sacrament.

Fraternally yours in
His Eucharistic Love,

Msgr. Pepe
Msgr. Pepe

COMPASSION

St. Patrick
March 17, 1994

J.M.J.

Dear Fr. Thomas,

Happy St. Patrick's Day! He is, of course, the patron saint of Ireland. Ireland is the most glorious of all the nations because the great Irish missionaries have evangelized the world. From such a small place, look at the tremendous impact that they have had on the Church in the spreading of the faith.

Indirectly, it was an Irishman who brought perpetual adoration to the Philippines. Cardinal Sin was invited to be the main celebrant and homilist for a Mass in honor of Edell Quinn at the International Eucharistic Congress in Kenya nine years ago. She was a great lay missionary who organized the Legion of Mary throughout Africa. The Mass was held at her grave. A group of women attending the Congress wanted Fr. Martin to attend. Instead, he wanted to take a siesta because the Pope just had a three hour Mass under the hot African sun. They insisted and practically dragged him with them on the long hike to the grave site. He went because he knew of Edell Quinn's great love for the Eucharist.

But, when he arrived he was too tired to stay. All he wanted to do was "escape" from the clutches of these women and return to the hotel to nap. He would vest, proceed to the altar, then, lost among all of the other priests, he would leave and make his way back to the hotel.

However, when Cardinal Sin started speaking, Fr. Martin was so moved by his homily that he decided to stay. After Mass Fr. Martin met the Cardinal who invited him to come to the Philippines to promote perpetual adoration where we now have over five hundred chapels.

The Cardinal began his homily by saying, when he was a little boy, his mother would come into his bedroom and kiss him goodnight, before he went to sleep. After the kiss she would lean over and whisper this in his ear: "Jaime, I love you more than all the rest." The Cardinal is one of eleven children. Each night his mother would do this until one night he asked her: "Why, Mother, do you love me more than all the rest?" Her reply: "Because you are the ugliest one I have."

This is funny. But it also speaks to us of the compassionate love of Jesus in the Blessed Sacrament. This compassion was portrayed by an Irish missionary working in Africa. He was chaplain to a men's prison. He received an obedience to return to Ireland, and I was with him for his last visit to the prisoners who, according to society, are the most wretched of all men.

After his last visit to the prison, we both got into his car to return to his parish. He put the key into the ignition, then put his head on the steering wheel and began to weep at the thought that he would never see these men again.

I thought that here was an image of Christ. Because He could not bear to leave us, He instituted the Blessed Sacrament, so that He could stay with us until the very end of time. The uglier and the more wretched we are, the more His tender and compassionate Heart goes out to us. The worse we feel ourselves to be, the greater joy we bring to Him when we humble ourselves and go to Him in the Blessed Sacrament. He is the Wounded Healer who has come, not for those who are well, but for those who are sick.

A sick little baby in California moved her parents to invite Fr. Martin into their parish to establish perpetual adoration. Ed and Sybella Alexander could not leave the side of their new-born Catherine. She was born premature and was so small that the doctors said she could not live.

So little, so sick, so helpless, their heart ached, for Catherine. Then they thought that this is how Jesus in the Blessed Sacrament must feel toward each of us. If they felt such unspeakable compassion toward Catherine, how much more is the compassion of Jesus in the Blessed Sacrament toward our frailty and sinfullness.

Through perpetual adoration, He ministers His healing love and grace directly to us. Msgr. Peter Memnaugh is Ed and Sybella's pastor at St. Vincent's in Mission Hills. He invited Fr. Martin to Ireland. Through the grapevine of Jesu Caritas priests, perpetual adoration spread throughout Ireland, beginning at the Cathedral of St. Mel's in Longford. Bishop Leopold Tumulok is a Jesu Caritas priest and has been most supportive and encouraging toward perpetual adoration.

Fr. Martin says that the Irish priests in America made the apostolate possible. Over one hundred Irish priests have started perpetual adoration in their parishes in the States.

The Irish preferred death to denial. Love for the Holy Eucharist and the Blessed Mother characterizes their deep faith. During the time of persecution they had 'rock' masses in the woods. If caught by the British they were killed. Love for the Holy Eucharist still inflames their faith.

No wonder Our Lady chose Ireland for the most Eucharistic message of all. Nothing was said. She was silent. She appeared with the Lamb. Apocalyptical time. Time for the Blessed Mother and the Blessed Sacrament. She is Our Lady of Knock.

Fraternally yours in
His Eucharistic Love,

Msgr. Pepe

Msgr. Pepe

A ROOM IN THE INN

Feast Day of St. Joseph, Husband of Mary
March 19, 1994

J.M.J.

Dear Fr. Thomas,

Today is the feast of St. Joseph. There is not much said about St. Joseph in scripture. He was a just and faithful servant, and a quiet figure in the history of salvation.

St. Joseph reminds me of the vast majority of Catholic priests in the world today. They are just, faithful and totally dedicated to God and the service of the church. Because they are not disruptive, they do not get any publicity. They are so pastorally oriented, busy taking care of the people in their parish, that nothing is ever said or written about how much they do for God and his people. Like St. Joseph, they quietly go about their life working for the glory of God.

Look to St. Joseph, Thomas, as your model. He represents spiritual and apostolic maturity. By maturity, I mean he was dedicated to the interest of Christ. He put the interest of Christ ahead of his own.

In his love for Jesus and Mary, his thought process focused on their needs, rather than his own. In theory, every priest would agree to this. In practice, however, it may be a different matter.

For example, I have asked many priests to consider having perpetual adoration of the Blessed Sacrament. Many of them say that they cannot find a place for a prayer room.

Did not St. Joseph search until he found a place for Christ to be born? "There was no room for them in the inn." (LK 2:7). But St. Joseph kept searching until he found a place. And this place he found in Bethlehem became the first chapel of perpetual adoration where even the shepherds in that region, living in the fields, came to adore Him.

A priest whose mind is primarily on the interest of Christ would give up his own bedroom, if there were no other place available, if it meant finding a place where the Blessed Sacrament would be adored day and night.

I know such a priest. He came to Manila for the ordination of Fr. Brian Morgan. His name is Fr. Brian Ahern. Fr. Ahern is pastor of St. Gerard's Catholic Church in Geraldton, Western Australia. Fr. Ahern wanted perpetual adoration in his parish, but there was no room anywhere for a prayer chapel.

Fr. Ahern did what St. Joseph would have done. He gave Jesus his bedroom. It makes an ideal chapel because it has a separate, outside entrance. One does not have to go through the rectory to come into the chapel. The privacy of the rectory is maintained as the people use the outside entrance to come into the chapel, which was formerly Fr. Ahern's bedroom. This can be kept warm during the cold Australian winter. And it is, also, small enough to create an intimate atmosphere for quiet prayer before the Blessed Sacrament.

Fr. Ahern moved his bedroom to another place in the rectory. The Lord says that in His Father's House there will be many mansions. I am sure that Fr. Ahern will have a very special mansion in Heaven for giving up his bedroom on earth so that Jesus could be adored day and night in the Blessed Sacrament.

Already he has been rewarded many times over. Fr. Ahern's prayer chapel inspired Brian Morgan to become a priest and to dedicate his priesthood to spreading perpetual adoration. Brian Morgan is now a priest. His holiness and love for the Eucharist has already attracted six other vocations to the priesthood. Five of them are now studying here in Manila at St. Vincent's in Tandang Sora for a new community of priests, Missionaries of the Blessed Sacrament, founded to spread perpetual adoration. These young men studying for the priesthood are Patrick Barry, Douglas Harris, Vincent Cherry, Athol Bloomer and Adam Hayward.

My consolation is that so many Filipino priests have found a room in the inn for Our Eucharistic Lord. They too will have a most special place, a most special mansion in heaven. They have a chapel of perpetual adoration in their parish so that Jesus can be loved and adored all the time by the people. These prayer rooms make it possible for the people to come anytime to be with Jesus. I am writing you this letter, dear Thomas, so that you may be the next one; the next St. Joseph priest to find a room in the inn for the Lord.

Fraternally yours in
His Eucharistic Love,

Msgr. Pepe

Msgr. Pepe

HIDDEN TREASURE

Holy Thursday
March 31, 1994

J.M.J

Dear Fr. Thomas,

Fr. Brian Ahern joined us tonight for Holy Thursday services. He is here from Australia to witness Holy Week in Manila. At dinner, he told me the story of Eileen Forth, a member of his parish in Geraldton. A similar experience also happened to Ann Lucia and Nancy Laneri.

Eileen left Catholicism and joined a Methodist Church. She said that God was not in the Catholic Church because there was so little enthusiasm for the faith.

One day she returned to the Church just to thank Fr. Ahern for all he had done for her while she was a Catholic. He was not at the priest house but at the Church getting ready for Holy Thursday Mass. She decided to wait.

After Mass, Fr. Ahern had a procession with the Blessed Sacrament. When the procession reached Eileen, who was sitting in the back, Fr. Ahern blessed her with the monstrance. She felt a tidal wave of love stronger than anything possible, but as gentle as a breeze.

Then she heard a voice:
"Eileen, I am in My Church. I am here truly present in this Most Blessed Sacrament. But people do not know Me or love Me and they leave Me all alone and abandoned. Help me renew My Church through Perpetual Adoration."

This is the same message that Pope John Paul II gave the Church on Holy Thursday night exactly fifteen years ago in his first encyclical *Dominicae Cenae*. In this letter the Pope said that "the Church and the world have a great need for Eucharistic adoration."

He called Eucharistic adoration "authentic renewal". And exclaimed that this was the very "aim" of the Council.

Pope Paul's *Mysterium Fidei* supports this. In 1965 he wrote this masterpiece because he said that his pastoral "concern" and "anxiety" was that the very hope of the Council was going to be frustrated. This hope was for "a new era of Eucharistic piety to pervade the whole church."

What happened was that Eucharistic adoration almost totally disappeared after the Council. *Mysterium Fidei* was prophetic.

In other words, once again the Apostles fell asleep when Jesus appealed: "Could you not watch one hour with Me?" Bishop Sheen said that this was the one specific request Jesus ever asked of His Apostles. He was denied then, and He is being denied by so many now.

This is why I don't want you to be asleep, but awake, alert and aware, dear Thomas. It is like the Westerner that Fr. Ahern met yesterday. This American, Norman Haynes told Fr. Ahern that he has been in the Philippines for over ten years looking for hidden treasure. He was very nice and said that when he found all of this gold, supposedly left by the Japanese during World War II, he was going to give it to the government to pay off the national debt and get the country out of poverty.

We were laughing about this when it struck me that the church world-wide was going through difficult times with division, demoralization, drop in membership and lack of vocations. Are we not becoming spiritually impoverished?

We would not have to search as hard as Norman Haynes to find the answer. The Blessed Sacrament is our Hidden Treasure! Now it is buried with neglect and forgotten in the Tabernacle. When we expose this Treasure of Love, with perpetual adoration, then we will become rich with the fullness of God's blessings and graces.

Fraternally yours in
His Eucharistic Love,

Msgr. Pepe

Msgr. Pepe

KING OF LOVE

Good Friday
April 1, 1994

J.M.J.

Dear Fr. Thomas,

When Cardinal Sin is praised for his many accomplishments, he jestingly relates the Biblical story when Jesus entered Jerusalem.

> "Jesus was riding a donkey when He entered the town. Naturally, the people started to sing while women spread their veils on the road where Christ would pass, welcoming Him in the name of God. "The poor donkey thought that all the ovations and praises were meant for him. He did not know that it was for Jesus, who was riding on Him."

We can all laugh at the humor of this story because it is reminiscent of human nature. For example, those who do not want perpetual adoration in their parish remind me of that donkey. They must think that all of the praise from the people is meant for them.

Or, do they think that Jesus does not deserve it? Perpetual adoration is praise for all Jesus has done for our salvation. Good Friday is the price that Jesus paid to institute the Eucharist on Holy Thursday night. First the banquet, then the bill. He gave up His Body on the cross for love of us, so that He may give His Body and all of His love to us in Holy Communion. The Eucharist is Jesus, King of Love.

On the cross, Jesus was lifted up in hatred because they did not want Him to be their King. "And they placed over His head the written charge against Him. This is Jesus, King of the Jews." (Mt. 27:37)

Through perpetual adoration, He is lifted up in love. From adoration of Jesus in the Monstrance, we draw down upon the parish and the world, the graces and merits of the Cross. I - once I am lifted up... will draw all men to myself." (JN 12:32)

By coming to Him in unceasing praise, we tell the world: This is Jesus, Our Adorable King of Love.

Through perpetual adoration we proclaim Him King by giving Him the honor He truly deserves. We take Him off the cross of shame, and replace the crown of thorns with a throne of glory by surrounding Him with love day and night.

When the whole Church proclaims Him King through a Eucharistic Renewal where every parish has perpetual adoration, then He will claim His kingdom and renew the face of the earth.

Fraternally yours in
His Eucharistic Love,

Msgr. Pepe

Msgr. Pepe

DIVINE MERCY

Easter Sunday
April 3, 1994

J.M.J.

Dear Fr. Thomas,

The main celebrant for our Easter Sunday Mass was Msgr. Moises Andrade. He was magnificent in singing the Exsultet and his homily was most inspiring.

Msgr. Andrade and I have been friends for many years. His great mind is matched with a greater heart. I mean he is very humble. His doctorate is on the history of the elevation of the Sacred Host. Another priest friend of mine thinks that he is the best liturgist in the Church today.

Tonight Msgr. Andrade significantly wore a Divine Mercy stole at Mass. There is a great connection between Divine Mercy and the Resurrection. Jesus specifically requested that the feast of Divine Mercy be celebrated on the second Sunday of Easter.

Here we have the culmination and conclusion of salvation history, Divine Mercy which is Eucharistically connected with Easter Sunday which is the Resurrection. This is because the final act, the greatest act, of God's mercy will be the manifestation of His glory from the Blessed Sacrament.

Now He is hidden in the Blessed Sacrament. One day He will manifest His glory and all nations and all peoples will see it. This will not be His Second Coming. His second coming will be like the sunrise. What I mean is the revelation of His Eucharistic glory will be like the first streaks of dawn.

The light of His glory will be His love and mercy. These are the two rays Sister Faustina saw radiating from the Blessed Sacrament. The white rays representing His Divine Love while the pink rays represented His Divine Mercy. These are the rays all humanity will one day see.

As Saul was converted by "a light" that "suddenly flashed around Him," (ACTS 9:3), so will the whole world be converted by the glorious light coming from the

Blessed Sacrament. This is what St. Peter calls "the coming of the great and splendid day of the Lord, and everyone shall be saved who calls on the name of the Lord." (ACTS 2:21)

Bishop Pierce lives in Providence, Rhode Island. After he retired as Bishop of Fiji, he was asked to translate the diary of Sister Faustina from Polish to English. He told me that the most outstanding vision of Sister Faustina was before the Blessed Sacrament.

With each holy hour made, rays would emanate from the Eucharistic Heart of Jesus and encircle the entire world. Every man, woman and child experiences a new effect of God's love and mercy for every holy hour made.

This is exactly what Jesus told St. Gertrude. One holy hour so touches His Heart that everyone experiences a new effect of His goodness in an explosion of Divine gratitude.

The effects of Mt. Pinatubo are still being felt thousands of miles away. Even sunsets in Canada are different because of its eruption. A chapel of perpetual adoration is a powerhouse of prayer exploding in graces benefitting all mankind. The effect and influence of a single holy hour of prayer is greater for the good of all mankind, than the extensive damage Mt. Pinatubo did worldwide.

A recent survey in the U.S.A. reported that only thirty percent of those attending Catholic Church on Sunday believe in the Real Presence. If it has happened to them, it can happen to us. Our people are becoming like Mary of Magdala when she came to the tomb. "They have taken the Lord from the tomb, and we don't know where they put Him." (JN 20:2)

It is up to us, dear Thomas, to tell our people where our Risen Savior is. The Blessed Sacrament is Our Risen Savior with all of the power of His love and mercy flowing out to those who come into His presence! This is where we must run, like Peter and John. This is where we must bring everyone. For each holy hour will advance the day when the light of His love and mercy will shine out, and then like Him, His people will be resurrected.

Fraternally yours in
His Eucharistic Love,

Msgr. Pepe

Msgr. Pepe

CROWN OF GLORY

Our Lady of the Blessed Sacrament
May 13, 1994

J.M.J.

Dear Fr. Thomas.

One morning when we were in Portugal, a kind priest showed us the crown where Our Holy Father placed the two bullets which had struck the Pope at St. Peter's Square on May 13, 1981. I thought this symbolized Our Lady's triumph. She will turn everything around and even the most vicious efforts of her enemies will be used to make even brighter, her crown of glory.

And according to our friend, Ging Roxas, Our Lady's crown of glory will be the Eucharistic reign of her Son. As you know, Ging is the expert on this Blue Book, and the main promoter of "Our Lady Speaks to Her Beloved Priests." Ging says the message comes down to this and is consistent with all of the approved Marian Apparitions in the Church.

The triumph of the Immaculate Heart of Mary will be the Eucharistic Reign of Her Son through the flourishing of Perpetual Adoration which will bring about the New Era, a second, a new, and a more glorious earthly paradise.

This is why the Holy Father was allowed by God to be shot on May 13th. It is the Feast of Our Lady of the Blessed Sacrament. The Pope is the Vicar of Christ. The significance of him being shot on the Feast Day of Our Lady of the Blessed Sacrament is this. It graphically illustrates the horror and evil of the unrelenting attacks on the Blessed Sacrament.

The world was in shock when the Pope was shot. What would be more terrible? As blatantly and tragically horrible as this scene was, of the Pope being shot, even worse is the unseen attacks of the One he serves so well, the Lord Himself in the Most Blessed Sacrament. Are we moved to do something about it?

Denial of the Real Presence, ridicule of exposition, and especially, attacks on perpetual adoration, are common place. Read the Book of Revelations and the battle lines of war become clear once you know that the "woman" is Mary against the "Dragon", Satan, fighting the "Lamb," Jesus in the Most Blessed Sacrament.

Who are the "kings" who "fight against the Lamb"? They are those in authority in the Church who fight against the Blessed Sacrament. But "the Lamb will be victorious because He is the Lord of Lords and the King of Kings, and those with Him are called chosen and faithful". (REV 17:14)

Nate Cortese is a friend of mine. His brother was killed during World War II. How many brave men in this century alone have fought and died for love of their country? How many wars have been fought for peace and freedom? And, yet, look how far we are away from either.

There is only one war worth fighting for. Larry Villone puts it best. "Standing up for Christ in the Blessed Sacrament today is like standing up for Christ when He was on the Cross!"

What we need today is an army of priests like you, dear Thomas, who are willing to fight, by standing up and being counted for the cause of Christ in the Blessed Sacrament.

The two men I admire the most are the holy Cardinal of Cebu, Cardinal Vidal, and our own Cardinal Sin of Manila. Cardinal Vidal said, if we do only what is ordinary, then we can expect only God's ordinary blessings. But because we live in extraordinary times we must be willing to do the extraordinary by having perpetual adoration in order to expect and receive what is most needed today, the extraordinary graces and blessing of God. Cardinal Vidal is working to bring about perpetual adoration in every one of his parishes.

My great joy as Vicar General of the Archdiocese of Manila is that Cardinal Sin has made it the most Eucharistic diocese in the world, with over 100 chapels of perpetual adoration. This is a tribute to a clergy most faithful to the Blessed Sacrament.

Be encouraged by the meaning of the miracle of the sun. Seventy-thousand people saw it October 13, 1917.

It was raining hard. A sign of tears, the copious tears of man's inhumanity to man. Mud was everywhere, like the corruption of everything we see today. Then the sun started to spin with the splendor of many colors coming down upon the earth. This foretells the coming glory of the Blessed Sacrament. The rain stops, the mud disappears and everything is made radiant.

Seventy-thousand people witnessed it, while the whole world will see this: "then I saw a new heaven and a new earth. The former heaven and the former earth had passed away ..... Behold, God's dwelling is with the human race ..... He will wipe every tear from their eyes, and there shall be no more death or mourning or pain, for the old order has passed away" (REV 21:1-4)

And Jesus in the Blessed Sacrament says: "Behold, I make all things new." (REV 21:5)

Fraternally yours in
His Eucharistic Love,

Msgr. Pepe

Msgr. Pepe

INNOCENCE

Beatification of Fr. Damien
May 15, 1994

J.M.J.

Dear Fr. Thomas

I wish you could have met Sister Gertrude while she was visiting from Hawaii. Even though she is over seventy, she is remarkable for her energy. She told me a story that has been a well guarded secret in her convent for many years.

When she was a young nun, one of the old nuns was dying. The custom at that time was for the community to gather in prayer around the one dying. Old, wrinkled, and ugly, the nun was breathing her last breaths. Suddenly, she opened her eyes, stretched forth her arms and exclaimed: " O My Beloved."

Then she sat up and gazed lovingly at the Blessed Sacrament, which she had permission to have in her room since she had been too weak to go to the chapel. What happened next had never been told, until Sister Gertrude shared it with me. The old, wrinkled nun changed to a strikingly attractive young woman, radiantly aglow with a countenance that put the rest of the nuns into ecstasy just looking at her.

After what seemed like a minute or two, the transformed nun went back against her pillow, turned old again and died. When the Sisters came out of their ecstasy, they were stunned to discover that this extraordinary event lasted for more than one or two minutes. The sisters were in ecstasy for over thirteen hours!

Sister Gertrude belongs to the Sacred Hearts Community, the same community that Fr. Damien belonged to.

Today the world knows that Fr. Damien will be beatified because of his work with the lepers. What the world does not know is Fr. Damien's devotion to the Blessed Sacrament, which empowered him to work with the lepers.

Fr. Damien volunteered to go to the island of Molokai, where lepers were ostracized from both family and friends because the disease was so contagious and, at that time, incurable. After Fr. Damien was there for a period of time a friend wrote him a letter and asked how Fr. Damien was able to stay so long among the lepers. Fr. Damien's reply was: "Without my daily holy hour in the Presence of the Blessed Sacrament, I would not be able to have stayed here a single day."

When Fr. Damien arrived the lepers did not notice. They were in a drunken stupor and had a sexual orgy each night to help them forget the rotting flesh of leprosy, dooming them to a life of oblivion and a death without consolation.

The first thing Fr. Damien did was build a chapel where he took each leper and the gospel scene was repeated over and over again: "A leper came to Him [and kneeling down] begged Him and said, 'If you wish, you can make me clean.' Moved with pity, He stretched out His hand, touched him, and said to him, 'I do will it. Be made clean. The leprosy left him immediately and he was made clean.'" (MK 1:40-42)

Jesus stretched out His hand and touched each one, making each one whole in His love, making each one innocent in His Blood. And innocence recaptured is more precious in the eyes of God than innocence never lost.

Oh, they kept their rotten flesh, but it didn't matter anymore. Their souls were made clean with the innocence of His Blood. They didn't need drink, because they became intoxicated with His love. Sex was no longer a need, because they had the intimacy of His Heart.

St. Francis kissed a leper. Through the grace of God he also cured one. Beside himself with pain, this leper insulted anyone who tried to care for him. He insulted Francis and Francis went before the Blessed Sacrament to pray. When he returned he said to the leper: "I shall do whatever you want." The leper replied: "I want you to wash me all over, because I smell so bad I can't stand myself."

Without hesitation, Francis had hot water brought to him, with sweet-smelling herbs soaking in it. As he began to wash the man, his rotten flesh regained its natural color and the leper was cured.

St. Francis is called 'God's Fool' because of what he did for the love of God. But far more foolish is the folly of love in the Blessed Sacrament because of what Jesus does for us. There He washes our soul, not in water, but in His Precious Blood. There we are made clean from the rottenness of sin and self love.

With each holy hour we make, He stretches out His hand and touches us. The more rotten we are, the more He takes pity on us. The more filthy we feel, the more He wills to make us clean.

Fr. Damien organized perpetual adoration in the chapel. Some of the best spiritual readings ever recorded came from the lips of these lepers in adoration. Fr. Damien would write it down and send it to his friends in Belgium and Holland. The inspiration is found in the charm of its simplicity.

One leper would spend his entire holy hour describing to Jesus what was dearest to his heart, like the sound of the waves, the blue of the ocean, the sunsets in the sky.

Only one man ever volunteered to help Fr. Damien, a man called Dutton. He came from Stowe, Vermont where Greg Lucia once gave his brother a book called The Virtue of Trust while visiting the Maria Von Trapp lodge. Dutton was agnostic and saw Fr. Damien only in a humanitarian light.

One day Dutton needed to talk with Fr. Damien and could not find him anywhere. Finally he went to the chapel to look for him. There he found him transfixed in prayer making his daily holy hour. Dutton concluded that Jesus Himself must really be present in the Blessed Sacrament for such a busy and dedicated man like Fr. Damien to take one hour each day to spend with Him. Dutton became a Catholic and the cause of his beatification is a possibility. A modern day Fr. Damien is Fr. Bill Petrie, assisted by his two sisters, Ann and Jan Petrie.

Sister Gertrude went back to Hawaii. I tell the story of the old nun for one reason. It's the story of each holy hour we make. If only we could see the change that takes place in us. We are made new in the Eternal Youth of Christ. We are made innocent, without blemish, as we are cleansed in His Precious Blood, in the folly of His unsurpassing love.

As the drop of water is cleansed and made innocent by the wine which becomes the Precious Blood of Christ at the words of consecration, so are we each time we come into His Divine Presence by the touch of His love and the Power of His grace.

Fraternally yours in
His Eucharistic Love,

Msgr. Pepe
Msgr. Pepe

SACRAMENT OF LOVE

Feast of Corpus Christi
June 5, 1994

J.M.J.

Dear Fr. Thomas,

Two years ago I was returning from a pilgrimage in Europe. A movie was playing on the airplane. I don't remember the name of it and I fell asleep before it ended. But one particular scene was noteworthy.

Robert Di Nero returns to his old neighborhood after a ten year prison term. He visits a schoolboy friend who now owns an expensive restaurant. As they talk he asks his friend about his sister. All during his prison term Robert Di Nero thinks about his friend's sister and wonders how long it will take for her to find someone else and forget him. As young people they enjoyed each other's company and loved to dance together. Their favorite song was "Ammapola."

But now things were different. He has been away so long, is a social outcast because he is a convict, and has no money in his pocket. He feels ashamed because he is a total disgrace, a misfit with nothing to offer her. Surely she is no longer interested in him and is probably married to someone else.

The brother told Robert Di Nero that the sister has not married and was, as a matter of fact, present at the restaurant that very evening. The brother points his sister out. Now that she is grown up, she is the most gorgeous woman that Robert Di Nero ever laid his eyes on.

The brother makes a signal to the orchestra as Robert Di Nero and the sister meet. They start dancing to their old favorite song "Ammapola."

Scared and nervous because he feels so inferior, he finally asks the question. "Please tell me. Was there even a time that you thought of me while I was gone?"

Her answer: "There was never a time I wasn't thinking of you while you were gone".

She waited and each day made her longing even greater. Why I write this today on the Feast of Corpus Christi, Thomas, is because of what Our Holy Father tells us about Jesus in the Blessed Sacrament. "Jesus waits for you with open arms in this sacrament of His love". (Dominicae Cenae)

In other words, Jesus is there waiting for you in the Blessed Sacrament. If He didn't care, he would not be there. It's like the old song says "If I didn't care ..... more than words can say ..... If I didn't care ..... would I feel this way ..... is this not love ..... for, if I didn't care ..... would it be the same ..... would my every prayer begin and end with just your name ..... be sure that this is love beyond compare ..... all of this is true because I care for you ....."

The purpose of today's feast day is to remind us of how much Jesus cares for us in the Blessed Sacrament. In the 13th century He appeared to Saint Juliana and showed her a moon with a dark spot on it. He explained that the moon represented the Liturgical Calendar and the dark spot represented a feast day that was missing that He wanted instituted.

Jesus said that as the church progressed in time, it would decline in faith in His Real Presence. This is in keeping with His gospel question of finding any faith at all when He returns. For this reason, He said it would be necessary to have a special feast day to remind everyone of His Real Presence in the Blessed Sacrament. St. Juliana remarked that there was Holy Thursday dedicated to the Eucharist. Jesus answered that Holy Thursday also celebrated the holy priesthood. He wanted a feast day exclusively to honor His Real Presence in the Blessed Sacrament. And that is how the feast of Corpus Christi came about.

On August of 1980 a major hurricane hit a city in Texas called Corpus Christi. We call it a typhoon. They call it a hurricane. It started in the Caribbean between two islands, one St. Vincent, the other St. Lucia.

Soon after the hurricane a very brave and courageous Bishop was named the ordinary of the diocese of Corpus Christi. His name is Bishop Rene Gracida. He writes this for Immaculata magazine,

> "On the occasion of an Ad Limina visit several years ago, our Holy Father, Pope John Paul II, made the statement that it must be very fortunate to be bishop of a diocese, the only diocese in the world, named Corpus Christi, the Body of Christ. I told him on that occasion, as I have told many others, that I do indeed feel very privileged."

Bishop Gracida was the first Bishop in the United States to invite the Missionaries of the Blessed Sacrament into his diocese. Many parishes in his diocese now have perpetual adoration as the result.

This invitation came about through a letter Kirk and Katie Pfeffer wrote to Rex Moses. Rex was working in the diocese with Operation Rescue. Kirk and Katie wrote Rex about perpetual adoration.

Rex showed the letter to Bishop Gracida. That is when the Bishop invited Fr. Martin Lucia and the Missionaries of the Blessed Sacrament into the diocese.

From Corpus Christi, Texas, the Missionaries were invited by four different Bishops to the State of Louisiana. From Louisiana to Alabama, Tennessee and Arkansas.

Through the super-dedicated efforts of lay people like Mary Ann Becksted and Pat Forton, they have been invited into dioceses from Georgia to Michigan.

When I think of the name hurricane, the wedding of Cana comes to my mind. To "hurry" the "wedding". Perpetual adoration will bring about and hurry the wedding between God and His people.

Fraternally yours in
His Eucharistic Love,

Msgr. Pepe
Msgr. Pepe

TENDER HEART

Feast Day of the Sacred Heart
June 10, 1994

J.M.J.

Dear Fr. Thomas,

On the Feast of the Sacred Heart last year, two friends, Meldy Cojuangco and Marietta Santos, took me to lunch at the Old Manila Restaurant in Makati. As we were talking, a few musicians with their violins, guitars and mandolins, were going from table to table singing songs.

When they came to our table they played a wonderful old song that I had not heard for over thirty years entitled "Remember When". A great melody with even better lyrics the song inspired a conversation on the Sacred Heart.

The Bible says God loved us before the very foundations of the world. The lyrics of this song express this:

> "Remember when? ..... I first met you .....
> I can't remember when ..... I didn't love you."

All of us know that when you love someone very much, you want to be with the one you love. A mother can hardly wait to hold her newborn infant. A father's joy is to be with his children. Friends treasure the moments they spend together. Sweethearts love so deeply they find it painful to part.

We know that the more one loves, the more one wants to be with the object of one's affection. This explains the very mystery of our Catholic Faith, the mystery of the Real Presence. Jesus stays with us day and night in the Blessed Sacrament simply because He loves each of us so much that He never wants to leave us.

Jesus exclaims, "Behold, I will be with you always, even until the end of the world", (Mt 28:20) Why? Because "I have loved you with an everlasting love and constant is my affection for you. Again I will restore you, and you shall be rebuilt." (JER 31:3, 4)

This is the message of the Sacred Heart. When I took a group of pilgrims to Paray Le Monial, this message was inscribed on the wall: "If you believe in My love, if you really believe in My love, then you shall see miracles of My love. I will reign in every heart and My victory shall be total and complete for I will reign through the omnipotence of My love in the Blessed Sacrament."

This is what Jesus told St. Margaret Mary to tell the world. The key word is "omnipotent", all powerful. She saw His Heart burning brightly like a million suns. His Heart in the Blessed Sacrament is on fire with love for each person.

This is why Jesus specifically requested, through St. Margaret Mary, that a feast in honor of His Sacred Heart be established in the Liturgical Calendar within the octave, eight days, of the feast of Corpus Christi. He wanted to make it unmistakably clear that devotion to His Sacred Heart is devotion to the Blessed Sacrament. The Blessed Sacrament is the Sacred Heart of Jesus living in our midst today!

His appeal through St. Margaret Mary is more urgent today than it was then: "I thirst with such a terrible thirst to be loved in this Most Blessed Sacrament." His message is that the Eucharist is not a thing, but a person, the person of Jesus Himself. In the Blessed Sacrament, He said we would find the most loving of all Fathers, our very best friend, with the tenderest of all hearts.

St. John Vianney saw with his very own eyes Jesus cup the face of each person who visited Him in the Blessed Sacrament and give each one a tender kiss of gratitude. "I draw them with hands of love ..... I fostered them like one who raises an infant to his cheeks". (Hosea 11:4)

This is the tenderness we find in the Blessed Sacrament from a Heart which is the most appreciative of our love. Jesus asked "Who touched Me?," referring to a woman who touched the tassel on His cloak. He wanted to know who touched Him because "power has gone out from Me." (LK 8:45, 46)

Power goes out from Jesus with each holy hour we make. Each holy hour touches His Heart and releases His healing love upon the earth until one day there will be a new and a second Pentecost.

The "fire" that will destroy the world will be the fire of Divine Love. The fire of His Heart will destroy the cold hatred of this world and establish the Kingdom of His Divine Love. (Pt 3: 10)

Perpetual adoration, Thomas, will be the cause and the catalyst of this cosmic event. God's love for man created the world. Only man's love for God in the Blessed Sacrament will recreate it "according to His Promise" where "we await new heavens and a new earth". (Pt 3:13)

From lunch at the Old Manila I went to the home of a poor family because the grandmother was sick and dying. I offered mass and there was one host left so we all decided to have a holy hour in honor of the Sacred Heart.

During the holy hour someone played a song from the house next door. Since it was hot and the windows were opened we could all hear it. The song was "Remember When". I haven't heard it since then.

But you can hear it with each visit you make to the Blessed Sacrament. His constant abiding presence is in itself a love song saying: I can't remember when I didn't love you."

Fraternally yours in
His Eucharistic Love

Msgr. Pepe

Msgr. Pepe

Birthday of John the Baptist
June 24, 1994

J.M.J.

Dear Fr. Thomas,

This letter is so important I am going to make it very short. I am willing to "decrease" the amount of words, in order to "increase" the impact.

St. John the Baptist's approach to Christ should be our approach to Christ in the Blessed Sacrament.

"There is one among you whom you do not recognize ..... whose sandal strap I am not worthy to untie ..... but the reason why I came ..... was that He might be made known ..... Behold the Lamb of God, who takes away the sin of the world ..... Behold the Lamb of God." (JN 1:26-36)

What we proclaim at the elevation should be the aim and focal point of our whole ministry: Making known Jesus in the Blessed Sacrament, whom so many do not recognize.

It's like my young friend Patrick Barry said to me recently. "Look in the gospel and you see that people were brought straight to Jesus. That is what we should do today, bring people straight to Jesus in the Blessed Sacrament. Where He continues to do for each one today, all of the wonderful things He did for the people in the gospel then."

Like John the Baptist pointing to the Lamb of God, the whole church should be pointing to the Blessed Sacrament. Like him, we must "decrease", that He may "increase" and establish His reign.

This is why the first apparition of Our Lady at Medjugorje was on June 24th, the feast day of John the Baptist. Like him she is pointing to her Son in the Blessed Sacrament. And she wants us to do the same for she specifically asked for perpetual adoration of the Blessed Sacrament.

And that is why the sun in the sky is dancing, dear Thomas. And why so many see it like a host. The sun is pointing to the Son for everything in creation beckons us to come to Jesus in the Blessed Sacrament. The sun is also pointing to the Son because His glory is coming soon. His glory in the Blessed Sacrament is about to burst forth and when it does: "Blessed are those who have not seen and have believed." JN 20:29)

Fraternally yours in
His Eucharistic Love,

Msgr. Pepe

Msgr. Pepe

Missionaries of the Blessed Sacrament, Inc.
P.O. Box 1701
Plattsburgh, NY 12901
Ph (518) 561-8193 Fax (518) 566-7103
e-mail ACFP2000@aol.com
Website http://www.ACFP2000.com

Contact us for additional copies of this book and other Eucharistic Meditation books, as well as, a variety of other related materials. We are also able to assist you in starting Perpetual Eucharistic Adoration.

Please ask Mary, Our Lady of the Blessed Sacament, to help you perform a small deed so that something great from God may come to your parish through Perpetual Eucharistic Adoration of the Most Blessed Sacrament. Ask your pastor to begin having Perpetual Eucharistic Adoration in your parish.